Chains Through Centuries: From Ancient Slavery to Modern Workplaces

Shah Rukh

Published by Shah Rukh, 2024.

CHAINS THROUGH CENTURIES: FROM ANCIENT SLAVERY TO MODERN WORKPLACES

First edition. June 6, 2024.

Written by Shah Rukh.

Table of Contents

Prologue

Human history is a tapestry woven with threads of freedom and bondage, prosperity and suffering, power and subjugation. At the heart of this intricate weave lies the concept of slavery—a practice as old as civilization itself, yet persistently evolving to adapt to the changing contours of society. From the dawn of time to the digital age, the dynamics of control and submission have morphed, taking on new forms and manifestations while retaining a chilling constancy.

In the ancient world, slavery was an overt and brutal reality. Empires like Egypt, Greece, and Rome thrived on the backs of those bound in chains, their fates sealed by conquest, debt, or birth. These early systems of bondage were raw and merciless, characterized by physical punishment and relentless labor. The Pharaohs wielded their whips, Spartan masters exacted harsh disciplines, and Roman overseers exploited human life for economic gain and entertainment.

As centuries passed, the brutality of physical chains began to share space with subtler forms of bondage. The medieval era introduced serfdom, where peasants were tied to the land, subject to the will of their lords. The Age of Exploration and the transatlantic slave trade ushered in a new, devastating era of human commodification, where millions were uprooted from their homes and sold as property in distant lands.

With the rise of the Industrial Revolution, a different kind of servitude emerged. The factory floors of Europe and America were filled with workers, including children, laboring under grueling conditions. Although the chains were no longer visible, the shackles of poverty, long hours, and hazardous environments were just as binding.

In the modern era, the corporate world has transformed yet again the nature of work and control. The physical whips have been replaced by psychological ones—micromanagement, digital surveillance, and the unyielding pressure of the 9-to-5 grind. Employees find themselves navigating a landscape where the boundaries between work and personal life blur, sacrificing family and social connections on the altar of productivity and success.

"Chains Through Centuries: From Ancient Slavery to Modern Workplaces" embarks on a journey through this multifaceted history of human subjugation. This book traces the evolution of slavery from its ancient origins to the complexities of contemporary workplaces. It explores the persistent undercurrents of power and control that continue to shape our lives, urging us to reflect on the progress made and the chains that still bind us.

As we delve into each chapter, we confront uncomfortable truths and recognize the resilience of the human spirit. We uncover the stories of those who resisted and the movements that sought to break the chains of oppression. Ultimately, this book is a call to action, encouraging us to strive for a future where equity, freedom, and respect define our shared human experience.

Welcome to a journey through the ages, where the past illuminates the present and guides us toward a more just and humane tomorrow.

Chapter 1: Origins of Servitude: Early Civilizations and Slavery

The origins of servitude trace back to the earliest human civilizations, emerging almost as soon as societies began to form complex social structures and accumulate surplus resources. In ancient times, slavery was deeply intertwined with the economic, social, and political fabric of burgeoning civilizations.

One of the earliest recorded instances of slavery dates back to Mesopotamia around 3500 BCE, during the rise of Sumerian city-states. In this region, slavery was a vital part of society. Enslaved individuals were typically war captives, debtors, or criminals. The Code of Hammurabi, one of the oldest deciphered writings of significant length, provides insights into the legal aspects of slavery in Babylon. It outlines the rights and duties of slaves and their owners, indicating a structured approach to the institution of slavery.

Egyptian civilization also relied heavily on slavery. From around 3000 BCE, slaves were used to build monumental structures, including the pyramids. These slaves were often prisoners of war, although some were born into slavery. The Egyptians believed in a hierarchy where slaves occupied the lowest rung. Despite their low status, some slaves could attain relatively stable and even respected positions within the household or administrative systems, reflecting a complex relationship between masters and slaves.

In ancient Greece, slavery was an integral part of daily life and economy. The city-state of Athens depended on a large slave population for various tasks, including household chores, skilled labor, and even administrative duties. Slaves in Greece could be war captives, born into slavery, or purchased from slave markets. While Greek society recognized the humanity of slaves, they were still considered property.

Philosophers like Aristotle rationalized slavery, arguing that some people were "natural slaves," meant to be ruled over.

Similarly, the Roman Empire's economy and social structure were deeply rooted in slavery. By the height of the empire, slaves constituted a significant portion of the population. They worked in various sectors, from agriculture and domestic service to skilled trades and entertainment. The Roman legal system provided a framework for the treatment of slaves, including harsh punishments for disobedience. However, Roman slavery also had avenues for manumission, and freed slaves could attain citizenship and integrate into society, albeit still bearing the stigma of their former status.

Slavery was not confined to the Western world. In ancient China, during the Shang dynasty (1600-1046 BCE), slaves were used in agriculture, construction, and as sacrifices in religious rituals. Chinese slavery was often hereditary, and slaves were considered the absolute property of their owners. The Zhou dynasty (1046-256 BCE) continued the practice, but over time, slavery in China evolved with changes in the political and economic landscape.

In India, the practice of slavery dates back to the Vedic period (1500-500 BCE). Ancient texts like the Rigveda mention the existence of slaves (dasa), who were often captives of war. The Manusmriti, a key legal text, outlines various aspects of slavery, including the acquisition and treatment of slaves. Although slaves in ancient India were at the bottom of the social hierarchy, certain rights and protections were prescribed, reflecting a complex and nuanced system.

The African continent also has a long history of slavery, independent of external influences. In ancient Egypt, Nubian slaves were used extensively. West African empires like Ghana, Mali, and Songhai also practiced slavery. Here, slavery was often a result of war, and slaves were integrated into households and communities, sometimes even rising to significant positions of power and influence.

Slavery in the Americas, long before European contact, existed among Indigenous cultures. For instance, the Aztec and Maya civilizations of Mesoamerica and the Inca Empire of South America utilized slaves captured in wars or acquired through trade. These slaves were employed in various labor-intensive tasks, including agriculture, construction, and as servants. The status and treatment of slaves varied significantly across different cultures and periods.

As societies evolved, the mechanisms and justifications for slavery also developed. In many early civilizations, slavery was justified by religious beliefs, legal codes, and economic necessities. The enslavement of war captives, for example, was often seen as a humane alternative to execution. Debt slavery was another common form, where individuals who could not repay their loans were forced into servitude until they worked off their debts.

The impact of slavery on ancient societies was profound. It facilitated the construction of monumental architecture, the expansion of empires, and the accumulation of wealth. However, it also entrenched social hierarchies and fostered systemic inequality. The institution of slavery created a class of people deprived of basic rights and freedoms, whose lives were controlled and exploited by others.

Despite the pervasive nature of slavery in ancient times, resistance and resilience were also part of the history of servitude. Enslaved individuals often found ways to resist their bondage, whether through passive resistance, escape, or revolts. The famous Spartacus revolt in ancient Rome is a testament to the enduring human spirit and the desire for freedom, even under the most oppressive conditions.

The transition from ancient to medieval times saw changes in the institution of slavery, influenced by the spread of major world religions like Christianity and Islam, both of which had complex and often contradictory views on slavery. While these religions introduced new moral and ethical considerations regarding the treatment of slaves, they did not abolish the practice. Instead, slavery adapted to new social, economic, and religious contexts, continuing to shape human societies in profound ways.

Chapter 2: The Pharaohs' Whip: Slavery in Ancient Egypt

Slavery in ancient Egypt is a subject of considerable historical interest, revealing much about the social, economic, and political structures of one of the most iconic civilizations in human history. The institution of slavery in Egypt, often depicted through the imagery of the Pharaohs' whip, played a crucial role in shaping the civilization's grandeur, particularly its monumental architecture, agricultural economy, and hierarchical social structure.

The origins of slavery in Egypt can be traced back to the early dynastic periods, around 3000 BCE. Slavery in Egypt primarily resulted from war, with captives taken as prisoners becoming slaves. These captives were often from neighboring regions such as Nubia, Libya, and Canaan, brought back to Egypt following military campaigns. The status of these war captives was one of complete subjugation, and they were considered the property of the Pharaoh or the state. Over time, slavery expanded to include individuals who were in debt, criminals, and those born into slavery.

The daily lives of slaves in ancient Egypt were varied, largely depending on their roles and their masters. Agricultural slaves, who formed the backbone of Egypt's economy, worked on large estates owned by the Pharaoh, nobility, or temples. These slaves engaged in backbreaking labor, cultivating crops such as wheat and barley, tending livestock, and maintaining irrigation systems. Their lives were harsh, with long hours under the relentless sun, and they were subjected to the constant oversight of taskmasters who used whips to enforce productivity.

Construction slaves, often depicted in popular media as the laborers behind the great pyramids and other monumental structures, also endured grueling conditions. These slaves, both skilled and unskilled, toiled in quarries to extract massive stone blocks, transported them across long distances, and assembled them into the architectural marvels that still stand today. The construction of the pyramids, in particular, required an enormous labor force, with thousands of slaves working in coordinated efforts under the supervision of architects and engineers. Despite the harsh conditions, there is evidence suggesting that these workers received basic necessities like food, shelter, and medical care, which were essential to maintain such a vast workforce.

Domestic slaves, on the other hand, had a different experience. Serving in the households of the elite, they performed various tasks, from cleaning and cooking to childcare and personal attendance. While their physical conditions were less strenuous compared to agricultural or construction slaves, they were nonetheless subject to the whims and demands of their masters. Female slaves, in particular, faced additional vulnerabilities, including sexual exploitation and coercion.

The religious and administrative institutions of ancient Egypt also relied heavily on slave labor. Temples, which were centers of both worship and economic activity, employed slaves for a wide range of duties, including maintenance, food preparation, and participation in religious rituals. Administrative slaves worked in government offices, performing clerical tasks, managing records, and assisting officials in the complex bureaucracy that managed the Egyptian state.

Despite their low status, slaves in ancient Egypt were not entirely without rights or recognition. Legal documents from the period, such as contracts and court records, indicate that slaves could own property, marry, and even buy their freedom under certain circumstances. The concept of manumission was present, allowing slaves who had shown loyalty or acquired favor with their masters to be freed. Additionally, the children of freed slaves could integrate into society, gradually erasing the stigma of their former status.

The treatment of slaves varied significantly depending on their masters. Some records suggest that slaves who served in elite households or temples were treated relatively well, receiving adequate food, clothing, and shelter. In some cases, trusted slaves could rise to positions of significant responsibility, managing estates or overseeing other slaves. This relative mobility within the constraints of slavery reflects the complex social dynamics of ancient Egypt, where personal merit and loyalty could sometimes transcend rigid social hierarchies.

Religion played a dual role in the institution of slavery. On one hand, it justified and perpetuated the system; slaves were often seen as fulfilling a divinely ordained role within the cosmic order. On the other hand, religious texts and practices sometimes provided a framework for the humane treatment of slaves. The concept of Ma'at, representing truth, balance, and justice, was a core value in Egyptian religion and governance. This principle occasionally extended to the treatment of slaves, advocating for fairness and compassion in their handling.

The symbolic imagery of the Pharaohs' whip, often used to depict the harsh realities of slavery, also had deeper cultural and political connotations. The whip was a symbol of the Pharaoh's authority and the power of the state, representing both the ability to command and the capacity to enforce discipline. It was a reminder of the social contract in ancient Egypt, where the Pharaoh was seen as a divine ruler responsible for maintaining order and prosperity, even if it required harsh measures.

The legacy of slavery in ancient Egypt is a complex one. On one hand, it facilitated the creation of some of the most enduring symbols of human achievement, such as the pyramids, temples, and monumental statues. These structures stand as testaments to the organizational and engineering prowess of the ancient Egyptians. On the other hand, they are also reminders of the human cost involved, the countless lives subjected to toil and suffering in service of the state and its rulers.

Historical accounts and archaeological evidence provide a multifaceted view of slavery in ancient Egypt. Tomb paintings, reliefs, and written records offer insights into the lives of slaves, their roles in society, and the attitudes of their masters. While these sources highlight the centrality of slavery in Egyptian society, they also reveal moments of humanity, resilience, and the complex interplay of power and dependence.

The decline of slavery in Egypt began during the later periods of its history, influenced by changing economic conditions, foreign invasions, and evolving social attitudes. The conquests of Alexander the Great and the subsequent Ptolemaic and Roman periods brought new cultural and economic dynamics, which gradually altered the traditional practices of slavery. However, the fundamental aspects of forced labor and social stratification persisted, adapted to the new political landscapes.

Chapter 3: Bondage in Babylon: The Code of Hammurabi

The Code of Hammurabi, one of the oldest deciphered writings of significant length in the world, is a crucial artifact that sheds light on the legal, social, and economic conditions of ancient Mesopotamia. This set of laws, inscribed on a stele and various clay tablets, was enacted by the sixth Babylonian king, Hammurabi, who reigned from 1792 to 1750 BCE. The Code of Hammurabi provides a comprehensive glimpse into the nature of bondage and slavery in Babylon, illustrating the complexities of servitude and the legal frameworks that governed the lives of slaves and their masters.

The stele of Hammurabi, found in the city of Susa, is notable not just for its content but also for its physical presence. Standing over seven feet tall, the stone monument is crowned with an image of Hammurabi receiving the laws from Shamash, the sun god and god of justice, symbolizing divine authority behind the king's edicts. This imagery underscores the perceived sanctity and immutability of the laws, embedding them within the religious and moral fabric of Babylonian society.

The Code itself comprises 282 laws that cover a vast array of topics, including trade, property, family relations, labor, and criminal justice. Among these, several laws specifically address the status and treatment of slaves, reflecting their significant role in Babylonian society. Slavery in Babylon was multifaceted, involving domestic service, skilled labor, and agricultural work, with slaves being obtained through various means, including war, trade, debt bondage, and birth.

One of the notable aspects of the Code is its detailed stipulations regarding the treatment of slaves. Law 15, for example, prescribes severe punishment for anyone who helps a slave escape or harbors a fugitive slave, underscoring the importance of maintaining the integrity of the slave system. This law states, "If any one takes a male or female slave of the court, or a male or female slave of a freed man, outside the city gates, he shall be put to death." This harsh penalty reflects the value placed on slaves as property and the necessity of protecting this economic asset.

The Code also addresses the sale and purchase of slaves, emphasizing the legal and economic framework surrounding slavery. Law 8 deals with the certification and accountability of transactions involving slaves, stating, "If any one steal cattle or sheep, or an ass, or a pig, or a goat, if it belongs to a god or to the court, the thief shall pay thirtyfold; if they belonged to a freed man of the king, he shall pay tenfold. If the thief has nothing with which to pay, he shall be put to death." This provision highlights the stringent measures taken to safeguard property, including slaves, and the severe consequences for theft.

Slavery in Babylon was not solely an economic institution; it also had profound social implications. Laws 117 through 119 focus on debt slavery, where individuals who could not repay their debts were forced into servitude. Law 117 states, "If any one fail to meet a claim for debt, and he sell the maid-servant, who has borne him children, for money, the money which the merchant has paid shall be refunded to him by the owner of the maid-servant." This law acknowledges the familial bonds that could exist between slaves and their masters and provides a mechanism for the redemption of slaves, suggesting a degree of humanity within the otherwise strict system of servitude.

The Code also provides insights into the rights and protections afforded to slaves. For instance, Law 199 addresses the physical abuse of slaves, stipulating that "If he put out the eye of a man's slave, or break a bone of a man's slave, he shall pay one-half of its value." While this law clearly reinforces the notion of slaves as property with a quantifiable value, it also establishes a form of legal recourse for the mistreatment of slaves, albeit primarily as compensation to the owner rather than justice for the slave.

Another significant aspect of the Code is its recognition of the potential for slaves to earn their freedom. Law 282 states, "If a slave say to his master: 'You are not my master,' if they convict him his master shall cut off his ear." However, this law implies that there were circumstances under which a slave could challenge their status, suggesting that manumission, or the process of a slave being freed, was an established practice in Babylonian society. Freed slaves, or "mushkenu," occupied a distinct social category, enjoying more rights than slaves but fewer than free-born citizens.

The legal framework established by the Code of Hammurabi also extended to the familial and social relations of slaves. Laws 146 and 147 deal with the rights of female slaves who became concubines or bore children for their masters. Law 146 states, "If a man take a wife and she bear him children, and that woman die, then shall her father have no claim upon her dowry; this belongs to her children." This provision indicates the recognition of the offspring of such unions and their entitlement to inheritance, reflecting the complexity of social relations involving slaves.

The Code also delineates the penalties for sexual relations between free persons and slaves. Law 138 states, "If a man wishes to separate from his concubine who has borne him children, or from his wife who has borne him children: then he shall give that wife her dowry, and a part of the usufruct of field, garden, and property, so that she can rear her children. When she has brought up her children, a portion of all that is given to the children, equal as that of one son, shall be given to her." This law underscores the legal recognition of relationships between masters and their female slaves and the protections afforded to such women and their children.

The economic significance of slaves is further underscored by laws related to their productivity and contributions. Law 234, for instance, deals with the leasing of slaves, stating, "If a vessel owner allows his vessel to be caught by the enemy, he shall replace vessel and cargo and pay one-half the value of the vessel as compensation to its owner." This provision highlights the use of slaves in various economic activities, including trade and transportation, and the legal mechanisms in place to ensure accountability and compensation.

The Code of Hammurabi is not just a reflection of the legal norms of its time but also a window into the broader social and economic structures of Babylonian civilization. It reveals a society where slavery was deeply integrated into daily life, with slaves occupying various roles that were essential to the functioning of the state and the economy. The detailed regulations and stipulations regarding slavery indicate a sophisticated legal system that sought to balance the interests of slave owners with certain protections for slaves, albeit within a framework that fundamentally viewed slaves as property.

Despite the harshness of many of its provisions, the Code of Hammurabi also reflects moments of legal innovation and social complexity. The recognition of manumission, the legal protections against excessive abuse, and the acknowledgment of familial bonds between slaves and free persons all suggest a nuanced approach to slavery that went beyond mere exploitation. These elements of the Code offer valuable insights into the ways in which ancient Babylonian society navigated the tensions between economic necessity, social order, and human dignity.

Chapter 4: Greek Chains: Helots and Servile Labor in Sparta

The institution of slavery in ancient Greece took various forms, and among the most unique and significant was the system of helotry in Sparta. The helots were a subjugated population primarily originating from the region of Messenia, which the Spartans conquered in the 8th century BCE. Unlike typical chattel slaves in other Greek city-states, the helots had a distinct status that combined elements of serfdom, communal labor, and subjugation under a militaristic society. This system of servile labor was integral to the Spartan economy, social structure, and way of life, revealing much about the nature of power, control, and societal organization in ancient Sparta.

The origins of helotry lie in the Spartan conquest of Messenia. After a protracted series of conflicts, known as the Messenian Wars, the Spartans subjugated the native population, turning them into helots. Unlike slaves who were bought and sold in markets, helots were tied to the land and collectively owned by the Spartan state rather than by individual masters. This meant that while they could be assigned to work for specific Spartans, they could not be individually traded or sold away from the land they worked on. Their primary role was to cultivate the land, providing the agricultural surplus that sustained the Spartan economy and allowed the Spartan citizens, or Spartiates, to focus entirely on military training and governance.

The life of a helot was harsh and oppressive. They were required to turn over a substantial portion of their agricultural produce to their Spartan overlords, keeping only enough to sustain themselves. This system ensured that the helots remained economically dependent and politically powerless. The Spartans implemented numerous measures to keep the helots in a state of perpetual subjugation and to prevent any possibility of rebellion. This included a combination of psychological and physical oppression.

One of the most notorious aspects of Spartan control over the helots was the practice of the Krypteia. The Krypteia was a form of secret police composed of young Spartan men who were tasked with terrorizing the helot population. During their period of service, these young men were encouraged to kill any helots who were deemed rebellious or simply to reduce the helot population and instill fear. This systematic and state-sanctioned violence ensured that the helots remained subdued and too fearful to organize any large-scale resistance.

The relationship between the Spartans and the helots was marked by a constant tension and mutual distrust. The helots vastly outnumbered the Spartan citizens, which made the fear of rebellion a permanent concern for the Spartan state. This demographic imbalance necessitated a continuous and oppressive system of control. The Spartans justified their dominance over the helots through a belief in their own superiority and a militaristic ideology that valorized strength and conquest.

Despite their subjugated status, the helots played a crucial role in the Spartan military system. During times of war, the Spartans would often use helots as auxiliary troops. While helots were generally relegated to non-combat roles such as carrying supplies or serving as light infantry, there were occasions when they fought alongside Spartan soldiers. For example, during the Battle of Plataea in 479 BCE, helots fought with the Spartans against the Persian forces. In some cases, helots who displayed exceptional bravery or loyalty could be rewarded with freedom, though such instances were rare and did not significantly alter the overall system of oppression.

The economic contribution of the helots was indispensable to Spartan society. Their labor allowed the Spartiates to focus on their rigorous military training and civic duties. The Spartan education system, known as the agoge, required young Spartans to undergo intense physical and military training from a young age, leaving them no time for agricultural work. This system was only sustainable because the helots provided the necessary labor to support the Spartan economy. The surplus produced by the helots not only sustained the Spartan population but also supported the state's ability to maintain a professional standing army.

Helotry also had profound social and cultural implications for Spartan society. The rigid class division between the Spartiates and the helots reinforced a culture of exclusivity and militarism. The constant threat posed by the helot population necessitated a society that was perpetually prepared for conflict, both internal and external. This fostered a culture of discipline, austerity, and vigilance among the Spartans. The fear of helot revolts was a driving force behind many of Sparta's social policies and military practices.

The helots' status as a subjugated people also influenced Spartan political structures. The need to control the helot population contributed to the development of Sparta's unique system of governance, which included a dual kingship, a council of elders known as the Gerousia, and an assembly of citizens. The Ephorate, a group of five annually elected officials, held significant power and played a crucial role in overseeing the state's control mechanisms, including the Krypteia. This complex political system was designed to maintain internal stability and manage the constant threat of helot rebellion.

The helot system also had repercussions for Sparta's relations with other Greek city-states. The harshness of Spartan society and its treatment of the helots were well-known throughout Greece, often eliciting a mix of fear, admiration, and criticism from other Greek states. The helots' plight contrasted sharply with the more common forms of slavery in places like Athens, where slaves could sometimes earn their freedom and participate more fully in economic life. This difference highlighted the unique and extreme nature of Spartan society within the broader context of ancient Greece.

Over time, the rigid structures of Spartan society began to show signs of strain. By the 4th century BCE, internal issues such as population decline among the Spartiates, increasing economic disparities, and the constant pressure of maintaining control over the helots contributed to the weakening of Spartan power. The helot system, which had once been a source of strength, became a liability. The decline culminated in significant defeats, such as the Battle of Leuctra in 371 BCE, where the Thebans, under Epaminondas, decisively defeated the Spartan army and liberated Messenia, ending the helot system in that region.

Despite their subjugation, the helots left a lasting impact on Spartan society and on the broader historical narrative of ancient Greece. The system of helotry offers valuable insights into the complexities of ancient slavery, revealing how systems of servitude could vary widely even within a relatively small geographical area. The helots' existence and the measures taken to control them highlight the ways in which slavery and subjugation can shape societal structures, influence cultural practices, and drive political developments.

Chapter 5: Slavery in the Roman Empire

Slavery in the Roman Empire was a complex and multifaceted institution, deeply embedded in the social, economic, and political fabric of Roman society. From its origins in the early Republic to its zenith during the height of the Empire, slavery in Rome evolved into a highly organized system that permeated almost every aspect of life. This intricate system of human property, where individuals were reduced to the status of commodities, played a crucial role in the development and maintenance of Roman power and wealth.

The origins of Roman slavery can be traced back to the early days of the Roman Republic, around the 6th century BCE. Initially, slaves were primarily war captives, captured during Rome's early territorial expansions. As Rome's military campaigns grew in scale and frequency, so did the number of slaves. Conquests in regions such as Gaul, Greece, and the Eastern Mediterranean brought in a continuous influx of enslaved people. These captives were typically sold in public markets and could be purchased by anyone with sufficient wealth, ranging from private citizens to the state itself.

The slave population in Rome was incredibly diverse, comprising people from all corners of the known world. This diversity included not only those captured in battle but also individuals who had been kidnapped by pirates, children born to enslaved mothers (vernae), and those who had fallen into debt and were sold into slavery. The wide variety of backgrounds among slaves meant that Roman society had to develop a range of practices and norms to manage such a heterogeneous group.

The roles and functions of slaves in the Roman Empire were as varied as their origins. At the lowest end of the spectrum were the agricultural slaves, who formed the backbone of the Roman economy. These slaves worked on large estates, known as latifundia, which were owned by wealthy Roman elites. Agricultural slaves performed grueling labor, cultivating crops such as wheat, olives, and grapes, which were essential to Rome's food supply and trade economy. The conditions on these estates were harsh, with slaves often working from dawn until dusk under the supervision of overseers who wielded significant power over their lives.

Urban slavery in Rome presented a different set of conditions and opportunities. Domestic slaves in Roman households performed a wide array of tasks, from cooking and cleaning to tutoring children and managing household affairs. In the homes of the wealthy, slaves could attain specialized roles such as secretaries, accountants, and even physicians. While these positions often offered better living conditions and a higher status than agricultural labor, domestic slaves were still subject to the whims and abuses of their masters.

The use of slaves extended beyond the private sphere into public works and infrastructure. Slaves were employed in the construction and maintenance of roads, aqueducts, and public buildings. They also worked in mines and quarries, extracting valuable resources like gold, silver, and marble. The labor in these sectors was exceedingly brutal and dangerous, with high mortality rates due to the hazardous conditions. Nonetheless, this exploitation was crucial for the expansion and maintenance of the Roman Empire's vast infrastructure.

Another significant area where slaves were employed was in entertainment and spectacle. Gladiators, often slaves or condemned criminals, were trained to fight in arenas for the amusement of the Roman populace. These gladiatorial games were a central aspect of Roman culture, symbolizing the might and dominance of Rome. Although the life of a gladiator was fraught with danger, those who achieved success in the arena could sometimes gain fame, wealth, and even freedom.

The legal framework surrounding slavery in Rome was complex and codified through a series of laws and edicts. Slaves were considered property (res) under Roman law, lacking personal rights and subject to the absolute authority of their masters. The power of a master over his slaves (dominium) included the right to punish, sell, or even kill them. However, there were certain legal protections in place, albeit minimal. For example, the killing of a slave without cause could lead to legal repercussions, though these laws were often more concerned with property damage than with the welfare of the slave.

Manumission, the act of freeing a slave, was a common practice in Rome and could be achieved through various means. A slave could be freed by their master as a reward for loyal service, through a provision in the master's will, or by purchasing their own freedom if they had saved enough money. Freed slaves, known as liberti or freedmen, occupied a unique social position. While they were not granted full citizenship, they could engage in business, own property, and participate in certain civic activities. The children of freedmen, however, were born as full Roman citizens, illustrating a path of upward mobility that was embedded within the system of slavery.

The economic impact of slavery on the Roman Empire was profound. Slaves were a vital component of the Roman economy, driving agricultural production, supporting urban industries, and contributing to the state's wealth through their labor. The availability of cheap slave labor allowed Roman elites to amass vast fortunes, which they used to fund public works, military campaigns, and their own luxurious lifestyles. The reliance on slaves also affected social dynamics, as the disparity between the wealthy elite and the poor free citizens grew wider, contributing to social tensions and unrest.

Culturally, the presence of slavery influenced Roman attitudes and values. The institution of slavery reinforced notions of hierarchy and dominance, which were central to Roman identity. Slaves were often depicted in literature and art as inferior beings, their subjugation serving as a reminder of Roman superiority and power. This cultural perspective permeated various aspects of Roman life, from household management to military conquests, where the subjugation of others was both a practical necessity and a symbol of Rome's greatness.

Despite the pervasive nature of slavery, there were moments of resistance and rebellion. The most famous of these was the Spartacus Rebellion (73-71 BCE), led by the gladiator Spartacus. This massive slave uprising posed a significant threat to Roman stability and required substantial military force to suppress. The rebellion highlighted the inherent tensions within the system of slavery and the potential for widespread unrest among the enslaved population.

The decline of slavery in the Roman Empire was gradual and linked to broader economic and social transformations. As the empire faced increasing external pressures and internal decay, the economic foundations that supported large-scale slavery began to weaken. Additionally, the rise of Christianity introduced new moral and ethical perspectives on slavery. Early Christian teachings often advocated for more humane treatment of slaves and emphasized the spiritual equality of all individuals. While these teachings did not immediately dismantle the institution of slavery, they contributed to a gradual shift in attitudes that would eventually lead to its decline.

By the late Roman Empire, the institution of slavery was evolving. The economic importance of slaves diminished as other forms of labor, such as serfdom, began to emerge. The transformation of Roman society, coupled with the administrative and military challenges facing the empire, led to a gradual erosion of the traditional system of slavery. By the early Middle Ages, the dynamics of servitude and labor had changed significantly, paving the way for new social and economic structures.

Chapter 6: Masters and Gladiators: Spectacle and Suffering

In ancient Rome, the relationship between masters and gladiators exemplified a complex interplay of spectacle and suffering, rooted in a society that prized both entertainment and power. Gladiators were typically slaves, prisoners of war, or criminals condemned to fight in the arena. However, some were volunteers who sought fame, fortune, or the thrill of combat. Regardless of their origins, all gladiators were subjected to rigorous training, brutal discipline, and the constant threat of death, reflecting the harsh realities of their existence.

The masters, or lanistae, who owned and trained gladiators, operated schools called ludi, where the fighters were prepared for the deadly games. These schools were more akin to prisons than training facilities. Gladiators lived under strict surveillance and were often shackled when not training to prevent escape. Their training regimes were intense, designed to hone their skills in various forms of combat, with different weapons and fighting styles. The training ensured that they could provide the best possible spectacle in the arena, meeting the Roman public's insatiable appetite for bloodshed and drama.

The life of a gladiator was one of constant physical and psychological torment. Injuries were commonplace, and medical care was rudimentary, focused primarily on getting fighters back into the arena as quickly as possible. The threat of death was ever-present, as gladiatorial contests were often fought to the death, especially in the earlier periods of Roman history. Even if a gladiator won his bouts, his life was still marked by violence and suffering, with each victory bringing only a temporary reprieve from the constant danger.

Masters exercised absolute control over their gladiators. They decided who fought and when, often pitting their fighters against each other or against wild animals in matches designed to thrill the crowd.

The lanistae had significant financial investments in their gladiators, and successful fighters could be quite valuable. Thus, while the masters were ruthless, they also had a vested interest in maintaining the health and skill of their best fighters. Nonetheless, the welfare of the gladiators was always secondary to the spectacle they provided and the profits they generated.

The arenas themselves were grand structures, capable of holding tens of thousands of spectators. The Colosseum in Rome, the most famous of these arenas, could seat around 50,000 people. These massive venues were architectural marvels of their time, equipped with elaborate systems to stage complex battles, including naval reenactments. The games were a significant part of Roman culture, serving not just as entertainment but also as a means of demonstrating the power and generosity of the ruling class. Emperors and politicians often sponsored games to gain favor with the populace, using the spectacle to distract and placate the masses.

The audience played a crucial role in the dynamics of the gladiatorial games. Their reactions could influence the fate of the fighters, with emperors and officials sometimes deferring to the crowd's wishes when deciding whether a defeated gladiator should live or die. The famous gesture of the thumb, though its exact nature is debated by historians, symbolized the power of the masses over the individual's fate in the arena. This interplay added a layer of unpredictability and drama to the games, enhancing their appeal.

Despite their status as slaves, some gladiators achieved a degree of fame and recognition. Successful fighters could become popular heroes, their exploits celebrated in songs and stories. They might earn prizes, money, and even freedom if they performed exceptionally well. The symbol of the rudis, a wooden sword, represented a gladiator's liberation, awarded to those who had shown extraordinary skill and bravery. However, such instances were rare, and for most gladiators, their lives remained harsh and short.

The suffering of the gladiators extended beyond physical pain. The psychological toll of constant combat, the loss of freedom, and the ever-present fear of death created an existence marked by terror and despair. They were forced to adopt a persona of stoicism and courage, traits highly valued in Roman culture, yet their inner lives were undoubtedly filled with turmoil. The bonds they formed with fellow gladiators, who were simultaneously comrades and potential opponents, added another layer of complexity to their lives.

Over time, the nature of the games and the treatment of gladiators evolved. By the late Roman Empire, the frequency of lethal contests decreased, and more emphasis was placed on skillful combat rather than outright killing. The growing influence of Christianity, which condemned the brutality of the games, also contributed to their decline. Eventually, gladiatorial games were abolished altogether in the 5th century AD, as changing societal values and economic pressures rendered them obsolete.

In examining the relationship between masters and gladiators, it is evident that the spectacle and suffering of the arena were inextricably linked. The masters wielded absolute power, driving their fighters to perform acts of incredible bravery and brutality for the amusement of the masses. The gladiators, despite their lowly status, became central figures in a grand cultural phenomenon that both celebrated and commodified human life and death. Their suffering, endured for the sake of spectacle, remains a poignant reminder of the darker aspects of human history and the enduring complexity of power, entertainment, and survival.

Chapter 7: Shackles of the East: Slavery in Ancient China

Slavery in ancient China, while not as extensively documented as in other ancient civilizations, played a significant role in its social, economic, and political landscape. The institution of slavery in China evolved over millennia, reflecting the complexities of Chinese society and the varying dynamics of power, labor, and human rights.

In early Chinese history, during the Shang Dynasty (c. 1600–1046 BCE), slavery was prevalent. Slaves were primarily prisoners of war, victims of raids, and those who could not pay their debts. The Shang Dynasty's ruling class employed slaves for a variety of purposes, including agricultural labor, construction projects, and domestic service. These slaves were often marked by their distinctive physical conditions, such as tattooed faces or shaved heads, which set them apart from free individuals.

The use of slaves for large-scale construction projects, such as the building of city walls and palaces, was a notable feature of ancient Chinese slavery. These projects required significant human labor, often under harsh conditions. Slaves, along with conscripted laborers, were forced to work long hours with little regard for their well-being. The physical toll on these workers was immense, and many perished due to exhaustion, malnutrition, and inadequate medical care.

The Zhou Dynasty (c. 1046–256 BCE) saw the continuation and expansion of slavery. The Zhou rulers, who overthrew the Shang, inherited and adapted many of their practices, including the use of slaves. Slavery became more institutionalized, with legal codes and social norms defining the status and treatment of slaves. During this period, slaves were used not only for labor but also for sacrificial rituals. Human sacrifice, often involving slaves, was practiced to appease deities and ensure the prosperity of the ruling elite. These sacrifices were brutal and underscored the dehumanizing aspects of slavery in ancient China.

Confucianism, which emerged during the later Zhou period, had a complex relationship with slavery. While Confucian teachings emphasized social harmony and hierarchical relationships, they did not explicitly condemn slavery. Instead, Confucianism reinforced the existing social order, which included the institution of slavery. Confucian scholars and officials often viewed slavery as a natural part of the hierarchical structure, with slaves occupying the lowest rung of society. However, some Confucian texts did advocate for the humane treatment of slaves, reflecting a nuanced perspective on the issue.

The Qin Dynasty (221–206 BCE), known for its unification of China under Emperor Qin Shi Huang, also utilized slaves extensively. The construction of the Great Wall and the emperor's mausoleum, including the famous Terracotta Army, relied heavily on forced labor. Slaves, along with conscripted peasants, toiled under extreme conditions to complete these monumental projects. The harshness of Qin rule, including the use of slave labor, contributed to widespread discontent and the eventual downfall of the dynasty.

The Han Dynasty (206 BCE–220 CE) witnessed a significant expansion of slavery. During this period, the Chinese empire grew in size and complexity, leading to an increased demand for labor. Slavery became more widespread, encompassing a diverse range of individuals, including war captives, debtors, and those sold into servitude by their families. The Han government imposed heavy taxes and conscription on peasants, driving many into debt and subsequently into slavery. This period also saw the rise of eunuchs, who were often slaves castrated at a young age to serve in the imperial court. Eunuchs held significant power and influence within the court, illustrating the complex social dynamics of slavery in ancient China.

The role of slaves in agriculture was particularly crucial during the Han Dynasty. Large estates owned by the aristocracy and the state required vast amounts of labor to produce food and other agricultural products. Slaves were employed to work these estates, often under the supervision of overseers who ensured productivity through strict discipline and punishment. The reliance on slave labor in agriculture contributed to the economic foundation of the Han Dynasty, supporting its military and administrative apparatus.

As Chinese society continued to evolve, so did the institution of slavery. The Sui (581–618 CE) and Tang (618–907 CE) Dynasties saw changes in the social and economic roles of slaves. The Tang Dynasty, in particular, experienced a flourishing of culture and commerce, leading to shifts in the labor market. While slavery persisted, there was an increased use of free labor and tenant farming. Slaves were still employed in households, agriculture, and state projects, but their numbers and roles began to change in response to broader economic trends.

The Song Dynasty (960–1279 CE) marked a significant shift in the institution of slavery. Economic changes, including the rise of a more commercialized and urbanized society, led to a decline in traditional slavery. The Song government implemented reforms that reduced the prevalence of slavery, such as encouraging the redemption of slaves and promoting free labor. However, slavery did not disappear entirely. It adapted to new forms, including debt bondage and the sale of individuals into servitude to pay off family debts.

Throughout Chinese history, the legal status and treatment of slaves varied significantly. Chinese legal codes, such as the Tang Code, included provisions regulating slavery. These laws addressed issues such as the buying and selling of slaves, their treatment, and their rights. While these legal codes provided some protections for slaves, they also reinforced their subordinate status. For example, the punishment for killing a slave was generally less severe than for killing a free person, reflecting the lower value placed on the lives of slaves.

The treatment of slaves in ancient China was generally harsh. Slaves were considered property and had few legal rights. They could be bought, sold, and punished at the discretion of their masters. Physical punishment, including beatings and mutilation, was common for disobedience or attempted escape. Slaves were often subjected to grueling labor, inadequate food, and poor living conditions. Despite these harsh realities, some slaves managed to gain favor with their masters and improve their conditions, though such cases were exceptions rather than the norm.

The end of the traditional slavery system in China came gradually. By the Ming (1368–1644) and Qing (1644–1912) Dynasties, the institution of slavery had transformed significantly. The Ming Dynasty saw a continued decline in traditional slavery, with the state imposing stricter regulations on the buying and selling of slaves. The Qing Dynasty further limited the practice, culminating in a series of reforms that effectively abolished slavery in the late 19th and early 20th centuries. These changes were driven by internal pressures, such as economic shifts and peasant uprisings, as well as external influences, including contact with Western powers and their anti-slavery ideologies.

Chapter 8: Bondsmen of the Desert: Slavery in Ancient Arabia

Slavery in ancient Arabia, a region encompassing the vast Arabian Peninsula, was a multifaceted institution that significantly influenced its social, economic, and cultural landscape. This institution evolved over centuries, reflecting the complexities of Arabian society and the interplay of various influences, including trade, religion, and warfare.

In pre-Islamic Arabia, slavery was deeply entrenched in the fabric of society. Slaves were obtained through various means, including warfare, trade, and piracy. Capturing individuals during tribal conflicts and raids was a common practice, and these captives were often enslaved. Slaves were also bought and sold in bustling markets, with major trading centers like Mecca and Medina serving as hubs for the slave trade. The Bedouin tribes, known for their nomadic lifestyle, frequently engaged in raids that resulted in the capture of slaves. These captives were either integrated into the tribe or sold to other tribes and merchants.

The economic significance of slavery in ancient Arabia cannot be overstated. Slaves played a crucial role in various sectors, including agriculture, animal husbandry, and domestic service. In the agricultural sphere, slaves were employed to cultivate crops, manage irrigation systems, and tend to livestock. The harsh desert environment of Arabia made agricultural labor particularly grueling, and slaves bore the brunt of this demanding work. Their labor was essential for sustaining the agrarian economy, especially in oases and regions where farming was viable.

In addition to agricultural labor, slaves were integral to the pastoral lifestyle of many Arabian tribes. They tended to camels, goats, and sheep, performing tasks that were vital for the survival and prosperity of their masters. The care and management of livestock required extensive knowledge and effort, and slaves often possessed specialized skills in this area. The reliance on slave labor for pastoral activities underscored the dependence of Arabian society on this institution.

Domestic servitude was another prominent aspect of slavery in ancient Arabia. Slaves worked in households, performing a range of duties from cooking and cleaning to childcare and personal service. Wealthier families often owned multiple slaves who catered to their various needs, providing a level of comfort and convenience that free labor could not match. Female slaves, in particular, were frequently employed as concubines, a practice that had significant social and personal implications. These women were often subject to sexual exploitation and bore children who might either be enslaved or integrated into the master's family, depending on the circumstances and the master's disposition.

The status and treatment of slaves in ancient Arabia varied considerably based on factors such as their origin, skills, and relationship with their masters. Some slaves, especially those who demonstrated loyalty and competence, could attain relatively favorable positions within their households or tribes. Trusted slaves might be granted responsibilities and autonomy, managing other slaves or overseeing important tasks. However, the majority of slaves experienced harsh and dehumanizing conditions, subjected to physical punishment, arduous labor, and minimal rights. The legal and social framework of pre-Islamic Arabia provided little protection for slaves, who were considered property rather than individuals with inherent rights.

The advent of Islam in the 7th century CE brought significant changes to the institution of slavery in Arabia. The Prophet Muhammad, while not abolishing slavery outright, introduced a series of reforms aimed at improving the treatment of slaves and encouraging their emancipation. The Quran and Hadith (traditions of the Prophet) contain numerous references to slavery, advocating for humane treatment and the gradual liberation of slaves. For instance, the Quran enjoins Muslims to free slaves as an act of piety and atonement for sins. This religious injunction led to the practice of manumission, where slaves were freed as a demonstration of faith and moral integrity.

Islamic law, or Sharia, established specific guidelines for the treatment of slaves. Masters were required to provide adequate food, clothing, and shelter for their slaves, and they were prohibited from overburdening them with excessive labor. Physical abuse was discouraged, and the freeing of slaves was highly meritorious. Additionally, slaves were granted certain rights, such as the ability to marry (with the master's consent) and to seek legal recourse for mistreatment. The concept of mukataba, or a contract of manumission, allowed slaves to earn or negotiate their freedom by paying an agreed sum to their masters. This contractual arrangement provided a structured path to liberation, although not all slaves had the means to take advantage of it.

Despite these reforms, the institution of slavery persisted in Islamic Arabia, largely due to economic and social factors. The demand for labor in agriculture, trade, and domestic service continued to drive the practice. Moreover, the expanding Islamic empire brought new sources of slaves through conquest and trade, incorporating captives from diverse regions such as Africa, Central Asia, and Europe. The trans-Saharan and Indian Ocean slave trades played crucial roles in supplying slaves to Arabian markets, with African slaves being particularly prominent.

African slaves, often referred to as Zanj, were brought to Arabia through trans-Saharan routes and coastal trade networks. They were employed in various capacities, including as laborers in agricultural estates, pearl diving, and domestic service. The harsh conditions faced by the Zanj laborers, particularly those working in the salt marshes of southern Iraq, led to the famous Zanj Rebellion in the 9th century. This large-scale uprising, driven by the brutal exploitation and mistreatment of African slaves, highlighted the severe conditions and resistance within the slave system of the Islamic world.

Slavery in ancient Arabia also intersected with the broader Islamic civilization's intellectual and cultural developments. Notably, the Abbasid Caliphate (750–1258 CE) witnessed significant advancements in science, philosophy, and the arts, often facilitated by the labor and contributions of slaves. Scholars, translators, and artisans who were enslaved or of slave origin played crucial roles in the transmission of knowledge and cultural achievements. The institution of slavery, while oppressive, also created a context in which enslaved individuals could rise to prominence through their talents and contributions.

The enduring legacy of slavery in ancient Arabia extended into later periods, influencing the region's socio-economic structures and cultural norms. The persistence of slavery well into the modern era reflected the deep-rooted nature of the institution and its adaptability to changing circumstances. Efforts to abolish slavery in the Arabian Peninsula gained momentum in the 19th and 20th centuries, driven by both internal reformist movements and external pressures, particularly from Western colonial powers and international anti-slavery organizations.

The gradual abolition of slavery in the Arabian Peninsula was a complex and multifaceted process. It involved legal reforms, economic transformations, and shifts in social attitudes. The decline of traditional slave markets, coupled with the modernization of economies and the adoption of new labor practices, contributed to the erosion of the institution. International treaties and pressure from global organizations played a significant role in encouraging Arabian states to formally outlaw slavery and integrate freed slaves into society.

Chapter 9: African Kingdoms and Captives

The history of slavery in Africa before the advent of European colonization is a multifaceted and intricate subject, reflecting the diverse and dynamic nature of the continent's societies. The institution of slavery in pre-colonial African kingdoms was deeply rooted in the economic, social, and political fabric of these societies. Slavery was not a monolithic institution but varied significantly across different regions and cultures, shaped by local customs, economic needs, and social hierarchies.

In pre-colonial Africa, slavery was an established institution long before the arrival of Europeans. African societies had developed their own systems of slavery, which were distinct from the chattel slavery that would later be imposed by Europeans. In many African kingdoms, slaves were integrated into the social and economic structures, performing a variety of roles from agricultural labor to domestic service and even military duties. The status and treatment of slaves varied widely, with some achieving significant social mobility and others enduring harsh conditions.

One of the most significant aspects of pre-colonial African slavery was the diversity of sources and methods of enslavement. War and conquest were primary means of acquiring slaves. Captives taken during military campaigns were often enslaved, serving as a source of labor and a means of consolidating power. This practice was prevalent in many African kingdoms, such as the Ashanti Empire in West Africa and the Kingdom of Kongo in Central Africa. The capture of slaves through warfare not only provided labor but also served as a way to weaken rival states and expand territorial control.

In addition to warfare, other methods of enslavement included debt bondage, judicial enslavement, and kidnapping. Debt bondage was a common practice where individuals or families who were unable to repay debts were forced into slavery. This form of enslavement was often hereditary, with the descendants of debtors also bound to servitude. Judicial enslavement occurred when individuals were enslaved as punishment for crimes. This practice varied across different legal systems in Africa, with some societies using it more extensively than others. Kidnapping, though less common, was another means of acquiring slaves, particularly in regions where warfare and judicial enslavement were less prevalent.

The trans-Saharan slave trade was one of the oldest and most enduring slave trades in Africa, predating the Atlantic slave trade by several centuries. This trade connected sub-Saharan Africa with North Africa and the Middle East, facilitating the movement of slaves across vast distances. The trans-Saharan routes were established and maintained by powerful empires such as the Ghana Empire, the Mali Empire, and the Songhai Empire. These empires played crucial roles in the slave trade, acting as intermediaries and suppliers of slaves to the Arab world.

The trans-Saharan slave trade was characterized by its complexity and scale. Slaves were transported across harsh desert landscapes, enduring grueling conditions that often resulted in significant mortality rates. Upon reaching North Africa, many slaves were further transported to the Middle East, where they were integrated into various sectors, including domestic service, agriculture, and the military. The demand for slaves in the Islamic world was substantial, driven by economic needs and the social structures that valued slave labor. The integration of slaves into these societies varied, with some achieving prominent positions and others remaining in perpetual servitude.

The East African slave trade, centered around the Indian Ocean, was another significant pre-colonial slave trade that connected Africa with the Middle East, South Asia, and Southeast Asia. This trade was facilitated by the Swahili city-states, which were powerful trading entities along the East African coast. These city-states, such as Kilwa, Mombasa, and Zanzibar, played pivotal roles in the capture, transportation, and sale of slaves. The East African slave trade was extensive, involving the movement of large numbers of slaves across the Indian Ocean to destinations as far as India and the Indonesian archipelago.

The East African slave trade was driven by the demand for labor in various sectors, including agriculture, mining, and domestic service. Slaves were employed on plantations in the Persian Gulf, on the island of Zanzibar, and in other parts of the Indian Ocean world. The conditions of slavery in this trade varied, with some slaves experiencing harsh treatment and others achieving relatively better conditions depending on their roles and locations. The cultural and economic exchanges facilitated by the East African slave trade had significant impacts on the societies involved, contributing to the spread of Islam and the integration of African, Arab, and Asian cultures.

The internal slave trades within Africa were also substantial, involving the movement of slaves within and between African kingdoms. These internal trades were often driven by the needs of powerful states for labor and military manpower. Kingdoms such as Dahomey in West Africa, the Kingdom of Kongo in Central Africa, and the Zulu Kingdom in Southern Africa all engaged in internal slave trading to various extents. These internal trades were complex and multifaceted, reflecting the diverse needs and practices of different African societies.

The Kingdom of Dahomey, for example, was notorious for its involvement in the internal and external slave trades. Dahomey conducted frequent raids on neighboring regions to capture slaves, who were then either sold to European traders or used to bolster the kingdom's own labor force. The slave trade was integral to Dahomey's economy, and the kingdom developed a highly militarized society to support its slave-raiding activities. The political and social structures of Dahomey were deeply intertwined with the slave trade, with the monarchy relying on the revenue and power generated by the capture and sale of slaves.

The Kingdom of Kongo, on the other hand, had a more complex relationship with slavery. While it engaged in the slave trade, the Kingdom of Kongo also developed systems for integrating slaves into its society. Slaves in Kongo could attain significant positions and were often assimilated into the family structures of their masters. The judicial system in Kongo also utilized slavery as a form of punishment, reflecting the diverse roles that slaves could occupy within the kingdom.

The Zulu Kingdom in Southern Africa, under the leadership of Shaka Zulu, also engaged in practices that involved the capture and use of slaves. The kingdom's expansionist policies led to the subjugation and enslavement of numerous peoples, who were integrated into the Zulu social and military systems. Slaves in the Zulu Kingdom were often used as warriors, reflecting the militarized nature of the society. The practices of the Zulu Kingdom exemplify the diverse roles that slavery could play in African societies, extending beyond mere labor to encompass social and military functions.

The impact of pre-colonial slave trades on African societies was profound and multifaceted. The capture and trade of slaves had significant demographic effects, leading to population displacements and the depopulation of certain regions. The demand for slaves also fueled conflicts and warfare, as states and groups engaged in slave-raiding activities to meet the needs of the trade. The social structures of African societies were influenced by the presence of slaves, with complex hierarchies and systems of assimilation developing to integrate slaves into various roles.

The economic implications of slavery in pre-colonial Africa were also substantial. Slaves provided essential labor for agriculture, mining, and other economic activities, contributing to the wealth and power of African kingdoms. The revenue generated by the slave trade enabled states to finance their military and political ambitions, reinforcing their dominance in the region. However, the reliance on slave labor also had long-term economic consequences, as it inhibited the development of alternative labor systems and economic diversification.

The cultural impacts of the pre-colonial slave trades were equally significant. The movement of slaves across vast distances facilitated cultural exchanges and the spread of religious and linguistic traditions. The integration of slaves into African societies often led to the blending of cultures and the development of new social identities. The presence of slaves also influenced the arts, literature, and religious practices of African societies, reflecting the diverse experiences and contributions of enslaved individuals.

Chapter 10: Vikings and Thralls: Norse Slavery

The institution of slavery in Norse society, known as thralldom, was an integral part of Viking culture and economy. Thralls, the Norse term for slaves, were essential to the social and economic fabric of the Viking world, which spanned from the late 8th to the early 11th centuries. The Viking Age, characterized by exploration, trade, and conquest, was also marked by the widespread capture and use of thralls.

The origins of thralldom in Norse society can be traced back to the earliest stages of Scandinavian history. Slavery was a common practice in many ancient cultures, and the Norse were no exception. The institution was likely influenced by interactions with other European societies, where slavery was prevalent. However, the Norse developed their own distinct system of thralldom, shaped by their unique social, economic, and geographic conditions.

Thralls were primarily acquired through raids, warfare, and trade. The Vikings, renowned for their seafaring prowess and martial skill, conducted numerous raids across Europe, targeting monasteries, towns, and villages. These raids were not only motivated by the desire for wealth but also by the need for labor. Capturing individuals during these incursions provided a steady supply of thralls, who were brought back to Scandinavia and integrated into Norse society. The British Isles, Frankish territories, and Slavic lands were frequent targets of Viking raids, contributing significantly to the thrall population.

In addition to raids, warfare between rival Norse clans and tribes also resulted in the capture of thralls. Prisoners of war were often enslaved, serving as a means of both punishment and economic gain. This practice was a common aspect of the inter-tribal conflicts that characterized much of Viking Age Scandinavia. Trade was another important avenue for acquiring thralls. The Vikings established extensive trade networks across Europe and the Near East, and slaves were a valuable commodity in these exchanges. Thralls were traded for goods such as silver, weapons, and exotic items, linking the Norse slave trade to broader economic systems.

Once captured or purchased, thralls were integrated into various aspects of Norse society. Their roles were diverse, reflecting the multifaceted nature of Viking life. In rural areas, thralls were primarily employed in agriculture. They worked on farms, tending to crops and livestock, performing tasks such as plowing fields, harvesting grain, and caring for animals. The labor of thralls was essential for maintaining the agricultural productivity that supported the Norse economy. In addition to farming, thralls were also used in other forms of manual labor, including construction and craftsmanship. They assisted in building homes, longhouses, and fortifications, as well as producing goods such as textiles and tools.

Domestic service was another significant role for thralls in Norse society. In Viking households, thralls performed a range of duties, from cooking and cleaning to childcare and personal service. Wealthier families often owned multiple thralls who managed the daily tasks required to maintain a household. Female thralls, in particular, were frequently employed in domestic roles, reflecting the gendered division of labor in Norse society. Some female thralls also served as concubines, a practice that had both social and personal implications. While concubinage could sometimes provide a measure of security and improved status for female thralls, it also exposed them to exploitation and abuse.

The status and treatment of thralls in Norse society varied widely, depending on factors such as the nature of their capture, their skills, and their relationship with their masters. Thralls were considered property and had few legal rights. They could be bought, sold, and punished at the discretion of their owners. However, the treatment of thralls could also reflect the economic interests of their masters.

Thralls were valuable assets, and their well-being was often necessary for maintaining productivity. As a result, some thralls experienced relatively humane treatment, with adequate food, clothing, and shelter. Others, particularly those employed in more grueling tasks, endured harsh conditions and physical abuse.

The legal framework governing thralldom in Norse society was detailed in the various regional law codes, such as the Gulathing Law and the Frostathing Law. These codes provided regulations on the acquisition, treatment, and manumission of thralls. For example, the laws stipulated that thralls could not be killed without cause and that they were entitled to some basic protections. Manumission, or the freeing of thralls, was a recognized practice, and freed thralls, known as freedmen or leysingr, could integrate into Norse society, although they often remained in a subordinate social position.

The socio-economic implications of thralldom were significant in Norse society. Thralls were essential to the functioning of the Viking economy, providing the labor necessary for agriculture, craftsmanship, and domestic service. The wealth generated through raids and the slave trade contributed to the prosperity and expansion of Viking settlements. The possession of thralls was also a status symbol, reflecting the wealth and power of their owners. This dynamic reinforced social hierarchies, with the ownership of thralls concentrated among the elite.

The institution of thralldom also had broader cultural and social impacts. The presence of thralls influenced Norse attitudes towards labor, freedom, and social hierarchy. The integration of thralls into Norse households and communities created complex social relationships, with bonds of dependence and obligation forming between masters and thralls. These relationships could be characterized by both exploitation and a degree of paternalism, reflecting the multifaceted nature of thralldom.

The decline of thralldom in Norse society began in the late Viking Age and continued into the medieval period. Several factors contributed to this decline. The Christianization of Scandinavia played a significant role, as Christian doctrine generally opposed the enslavement of fellow Christians. The spread of Christianity introduced new moral and ethical considerations that gradually undermined the institution of thralldom. The economic transformation of Scandinavia also contributed to the decline of slavery. The shift towards a more settled and agrarian society reduced the demand for slave labor, and the development of alternative labor systems provided new avenues for economic productivity.

Additionally, the increasing political centralization and the establishment of more structured legal systems in medieval Scandinavia provided greater protections for individuals and promoted the gradual erosion of the institution of slavery. By the end of the medieval period, thralldom had largely disappeared from Scandinavian society, replaced by other forms of labor and social organization.

Chapter 11: Feudal Bonds: Serfdom in Medieval Europe

In the annals of medieval Europe, serfdom stands out as a defining feature of the socio-economic structure, deeply intertwined with the feudal system. To understand the nature of serfdom, it's essential to explore the broader context of feudalism, which dominated the landscape of medieval Europe from approximately the 9th to the 15th century. This system was built upon a rigid hierarchy of obligations and protections, with serfs occupying the lowest rung of the social ladder.

Feudalism emerged in the wake of the collapse of the Roman Empire, filling the power vacuum left by the absence of centralized authority. Land became the primary source of wealth and power, and its control was vested in a network of lords and vassals. At the top of this hierarchy were the monarchs and high-ranking nobles, who granted large parcels of land, known as fiefs, to their vassals in exchange for military service and loyalty. These vassals, in turn, would sub-divide their landholdings to lesser nobles, who also pledged service and protection. This chain of allegiance created a complex web of relationships, with the serfs at the very bottom, bound to the land and its lord.

Serfs were not slaves in the classical sense, as they were not considered the personal property of their lords. However, their status was one of profound subjugation and dependency. Serfs were tied to the land, meaning they could not lawfully leave the manor without the lord's permission. This bond to the land was hereditary, passing from one generation to the next, ensuring a stable and predictable labor force for the lord. In return for their labor, serfs were granted small plots of land to cultivate for their subsistence, as well as protection from external threats, which were common during the turbulent medieval period.

The daily life of a serf was arduous and dictated by the agrarian calendar. Serfs were required to work the lord's demesne, the portion of the manor retained for the lord's own use, for several days each week. This could involve plowing fields, harvesting crops, repairing buildings, and other necessary tasks. In addition to this labor, serfs owed various rents and dues to the lord. These could be paid in the form of agricultural produce, livestock, or, less commonly, money. On top of these obligations, serfs were often subject to various arbitrary demands, such as corvée labor, which required them to work on the construction of roads, bridges, and other infrastructure projects.

Despite these onerous obligations, serfs were not entirely without rights. They were entitled to use the common lands of the manor for grazing their livestock, collecting firewood, and other purposes essential to their livelihood. The lord was also expected to provide justice within the manor, settling disputes and ensuring the enforcement of customary laws. This system of manorial courts was a critical aspect of feudal governance, allowing for a semblance of order and stability within the fiefdoms.

The relationship between lord and serf was thus one of mutual obligation, albeit heavily skewed in favor of the lord. This imbalance was justified by the prevailing social and religious ideologies of the time, which emphasized the naturalness of hierarchical order and the divine sanction of the lord's authority. The Church played a significant role in reinforcing these beliefs, preaching that each class had its place and duties ordained by God.

Over time, however, the rigid structure of serfdom began to erode. Several factors contributed to this decline. The Black Death, which swept through Europe in the mid-14th century, decimated the population, leading to a severe labor shortage. With fewer serfs available to work the land, those who survived found themselves in a stronger bargaining position. Lords, desperate to maintain productivity, began to offer better terms to their serfs, including reduced obligations and, in some cases, outright freedom. This shift was accelerated by the growth of towns and cities, which provided alternative opportunities for serfs and peasants. The burgeoning urban centers offered wages for labor, attracting many from rural areas and further weakening the feudal bonds.

Additionally, changes in agricultural practices and the commercialization of the economy played a role in transforming the landscape. The introduction of more efficient farming techniques and the expansion of trade led to a gradual shift from a subsistence-based economy to one increasingly oriented towards markets. This economic transformation diminished the lords' reliance on serf labor, as they could now generate income through the sale of agricultural produce and other goods.

By the end of the medieval period, serfdom had significantly declined, replaced by a more fluid and diverse labor system. In many regions, serfs had gained personal freedom, becoming tenant farmers or wage laborers. The remnants of serfdom lingered in some parts of Europe, but the institution had lost its centrality and coercive power.

The story of serfdom in medieval Europe is thus a tale of exploitation and endurance, of a system that sought to maintain social order through rigid control, yet ultimately succumbed to the forces of demographic change, economic innovation, and the relentless pursuit of freedom. The legacy of serfdom is a reminder of the deep inequalities that have pervaded human societies and the constant struggle for a more equitable existence.

Chapter 12: Captive Crusaders: Slavery and the Holy Wars

The Crusades, spanning from the late 11th to the late 13th centuries, were a series of religiously motivated military campaigns initiated by the Latin Church to reclaim the Holy Land from Muslim rule. While these campaigns are often remembered for their religious fervor and the cultural exchanges they facilitated, they also had a darker aspect: the widespread enslavement of captives. Slavery was an integral part of the Crusades, deeply embedded in the socio-political and economic structures of the time. The practice of enslaving captives was not unique to the Crusaders; it was a common aspect of medieval warfare, but the Crusades amplified it due to their scale and the ideological justifications provided by religious zeal.

The First Crusade (1096-1099), launched by Pope Urban II, set the precedent for the capture and enslavement of both Muslim and Jewish populations. As Crusaders advanced through the Levant, they encountered fortified cities and towns, often leading to brutal sieges. The capture of Jerusalem in 1099, for instance, resulted in a massacre of its inhabitants, with survivors, including women and children, being enslaved. These slaves were seen as spoils of war, their capture justified by the belief that the Crusaders were waging a holy war against infidels. The enslavement of captives served multiple purposes: it provided labor for the Crusaders, disrupted the socio-economic structure of the Muslim territories, and was seen as a legitimate form of retribution and deterrence against Muslim resistance.

Slavery during the Crusades was not limited to Muslims and Jews. The Byzantine Empire, a Christian state, also suffered from the Crusaders' actions, particularly during the Fourth Crusade (1202-1204). The sacking of Constantinople in 1204, driven by political and economic motives rather than religious ones, led to the enslavement of many Byzantine citizens. This event highlighted the complex motivations behind the Crusades and the indiscriminate nature of enslavement practices. The economic benefits of slavery were substantial. Captives could be sold in burgeoning slave markets throughout Europe and the Middle East, generating significant profits for Crusader leaders and financing their military endeavors. These markets were well-established by the time of the Crusades, with Venice and Genoa becoming prominent centers for the trade of slaves captured in the Holy Land. The demand for slaves was high, and their labor was utilized in a variety of sectors, including agriculture, construction, and domestic service.

The treatment of slaves varied widely. Some were integrated into households and could eventually gain a degree of autonomy or even freedom through conversion to Christianity or by proving their loyalty and utility to their masters. However, many endured harsh conditions, with little hope of liberation. The theological justification for the enslavement of non-Christians was rooted in the medieval Church's interpretation of biblical texts and the writings of influential theologians such as St. Augustine. These sources were used to argue that the enslavement of infidels was a legitimate means of both punishment and conversion. The capture and enslavement of Muslims and Jews were seen as part of a broader divine plan to spread Christianity and reclaim sacred territories. This ideological framework provided a powerful moral justification for the often-brutal actions of the Crusaders.

The impact of Crusader slavery extended beyond the immediate physical and psychological suffering of the captives. It disrupted families and communities, exacerbating the social and economic instability in the affected regions. The constant threat of enslavement loomed over the populations of the Holy Land, contributing to an atmosphere of fear and resistance. Muslim and Jewish communities responded in various ways to the threat of Crusader enslavement. Some fortified their cities and formed military alliances to resist the invaders, while others sought refuge in more secure regions. The enduring memory of Crusader atrocities, including enslavement, fueled animosity and distrust between Christians and Muslims, shaping inter-religious relations for centuries.

Despite the prevalent practice of slavery during the Crusades, there were also instances of resistance and negotiation. Captives sometimes managed to escape or were ransomed by their families and communities. The ransom system became an important aspect of warfare during the Crusades, with both sides capturing high-value individuals and negotiating their release for substantial sums of money or strategic concessions. The economic and social dynamics of slavery during the Crusades were complex and multifaceted. The influx of slaves into Europe and the Middle East influenced local economies, labor markets, and cultural exchanges. While the primary motivation for the Crusades was religious, the material benefits of slavery provided an additional incentive for the participants.

The legacy of slavery during the Crusades is a testament to the darker aspects of this tumultuous period. It highlights the intersection of religious zeal, economic gain, and human suffering that characterized much of medieval warfare. The practice of enslaving captives during the Crusades was a reflection of broader societal norms and values, which accepted and often justified the subjugation of perceived enemies. As historians continue to study this era, the narratives of those who were enslaved and their enduring struggles for freedom and dignity remain an essential part of understanding the full impact of the Crusades on medieval society.

The end of the Crusades did not mark the end of slavery in the regions involved. The legacy of Crusader enslavement practices persisted, influencing subsequent interactions between Christian and Muslim powers. The Mediterranean slave trade continued to thrive, with European and Middle Eastern markets remaining interconnected through the exchange of human lives. The ideological justifications for slavery evolved but continued to be influenced by the religious and cultural conflicts that had been exacerbated by the Crusades. In examining the history of slavery during the Crusades, it is crucial to recognize the resilience and agency of those who were enslaved. Despite the oppressive conditions, many captives found ways to resist, adapt, and survive. Their stories, often overshadowed by the grand narratives of battles and conquests, provide a vital perspective on the human cost of the Crusades and the enduring impact of slavery on medieval societies.

Chapter 13: Conquistadors' Chains: Slavery in the New World

The arrival of the Spanish conquistadors in the New World in the late 15th and early 16th centuries marked the beginning of an era of profound transformation and exploitation, characterized by the widespread enslavement of indigenous populations and the later importation of African slaves. The conquistadors, driven by the desire for wealth, glory, and the expansion of the Spanish Empire, initiated a brutal regime of conquest and colonization that had devastating effects on the native populations of the Americas. The system of slavery that emerged during this period was marked by extreme violence, economic exploitation, and the imposition of a rigid racial hierarchy that would shape the social and economic structures of the New World for centuries to come.

The initial encounters between the Spanish explorers and the indigenous peoples were often violent. Christopher Columbus, during his voyages to the Caribbean, quickly recognized the potential for exploiting the native populations for labor. In his quest for gold and other valuable resources, Columbus and his men enslaved numerous indigenous people, forcing them to work in mines and plantations. This early system of enslavement was formalized through the encomienda system, a feudal-like arrangement wherein Spanish colonists were granted the right to extract labor and tribute from indigenous communities in exchange for providing protection and religious instruction. In practice, the encomienda system resulted in the severe exploitation and abuse of the native populations. Encomenderos, or holders of encomiendas, subjected the indigenous people to grueling labor, often under brutal conditions. The forced labor was primarily used for mining, particularly in places like Hispaniola (modern-day Haiti and the Dominican Republic) and later in the rich silver mines of Mexico and Peru. The encomienda system led to significant demographic collapse among the indigenous populations due to overwork, malnutrition, and diseases brought by the Europeans, to which the natives had no immunity.

The decimation of the indigenous populations prompted the Spanish crown to institute reforms aimed at curbing the worst abuses of the encomienda system. The most notable of these were the New Laws of 1542, which sought to protect the rights of the indigenous people and phase out the encomienda system. However, enforcement was weak, and many encomenderos ignored or circumvented the laws. The reforms did little to alleviate the suffering of the indigenous populations, who continued to be exploited in various forms of coerced labor.

As the demand for labor in the New World grew, particularly in the sugar plantations and mines, the Spanish and Portuguese turned to the transatlantic slave trade to meet their needs. The importation of African slaves began in the early 16th century and rapidly increased over the following centuries. The African slave trade was characterized by its sheer scale and brutality. Captured African men, women, and children were transported across the Atlantic in horrific conditions, packed tightly into ships where many perished from disease, malnutrition, and mistreatment. Upon arrival in the New World, they were sold into slavery and subjected to harsh conditions on plantations, in mines, and as domestic servants.

The integration of African slaves into the colonial economy profoundly altered the social fabric of the New World. The use of African slaves became especially prevalent in the Caribbean and Brazil, where the cultivation of sugar cane required a large and continuous supply of labor. Sugar plantations were notoriously labor-intensive and brutal, with slaves working long hours in the scorching heat under the constant threat of physical punishment. The life expectancy of a slave on a sugar plantation was tragically short due to the harsh working conditions, disease, and malnutrition.

The Spanish and Portuguese colonies also saw the rise of a complex racial hierarchy known as the caste system, which stratified society based on racial and ethnic background. At the top of this hierarchy were the Europeans, followed by mixed-race individuals (mestizos and mulattoes), with Africans and indigenous peoples at the bottom. This rigid system of social stratification was enforced through laws and customs that perpetuated discrimination and inequality. The racial caste system served to justify and maintain the exploitation and oppression of non-European populations. It institutionalized the idea of racial superiority and inferiority, with Europeans claiming dominance and control over the economic and social resources of the colonies. This system of racial hierarchy and slavery was not static; it evolved over time, influenced by economic needs, demographic changes, and resistance from the enslaved populations.

Resistance to slavery in the New World took many forms, from everyday acts of defiance to organized rebellions. Enslaved Africans and indigenous people frequently resisted their oppressors through work slowdowns, sabotage, escape, and the formation of maroon communities—settlements of escaped slaves who established their own autonomous communities in remote areas. One of the most significant slave rebellions in the New World was the Haitian Revolution (1791-1804), in which enslaved Africans in the French colony of Saint-Domingue successfully revolted against their masters, leading to the abolition of slavery and the establishment of the first independent black republic in the Americas.

The impact of slavery on the New World was profound and far-reaching. It shaped the economic, social, and political development of the colonies, creating a legacy of racial inequality and injustice that persists to this day. The wealth generated by slave labor fueled the growth of European economies and contributed to the rise of global capitalism. The human cost of this system, however, was immense, with millions of Africans and indigenous people subjected to unimaginable suffering and deprivation.

The abolition of slavery in the New World was a gradual and uneven process, influenced by economic changes, political movements, and the persistent resistance of the enslaved. The abolitionist movement gained momentum in the late 18th and 19th centuries, driven by moral, religious, and humanitarian arguments against the institution of slavery. The British Empire abolished the transatlantic slave trade in 1807 and slavery itself in 1833. Other countries followed suit, with varying timelines and degrees of enforcement. In the United States, the abolition of slavery was achieved through a bloody civil war, culminating in the Emancipation Proclamation of 1863 and the passage of the 13th Amendment in 1865.

In Latin America, the abolition of slavery was also a protracted process. Countries like Mexico and Chile abolished slavery in the early 19th century, while Brazil, which had the largest population of enslaved Africans in the Americas, did not abolish slavery until 1888. The end of slavery did not mean the end of racial discrimination and economic exploitation. Former slaves and their descendants continued to face significant challenges, including limited access to education, land, and economic opportunities. The legacy of slavery has had a lasting impact on the social and economic structures of the New World, contributing to persistent racial inequalities and social tensions.

The history of slavery in the New World is a complex and multifaceted story of exploitation, resistance, and resilience. It is a story that underscores the capacity for human cruelty and the enduring struggle for freedom and justice. Understanding this history is essential for comprehending the profound and lasting effects of slavery on the Americas and for addressing the continuing legacy of racial inequality and injustice in our societies today. The conquistadors' chains may have been broken, but the echoes of their impact continue to reverberate through the centuries, reminding us of the need for ongoing vigilance and commitment to human rights and equality.

54

Chapter 14: The Middle Passage: Transatlantic Slave Trade

The Middle Passage was the harrowing sea journey endured by enslaved Africans who were forcibly transported across the Atlantic Ocean to the Americas. This passage formed the middle leg of the triangular trade route that connected Europe, Africa, and the Americas. This journey was a central component of the transatlantic slave trade, which spanned from the 16th to the 19th centuries and was one of the most devastating and inhumane practices in human history. The Middle Passage was marked by extreme brutality, suffering, and death, with millions of Africans losing their lives or being permanently scarred by the experience.

The transatlantic slave trade began in the early 1500s as European powers sought to exploit the resources and labor of the New World. The demand for labor in the colonies, particularly in the Caribbean and the Americas, where plantations produced sugar, tobacco, cotton, and other lucrative crops, drove the need for a steady supply of labor. Indigenous populations had been decimated by disease, warfare, and harsh working conditions, leading European colonizers to turn to Africa as a source of labor.

The process of capturing and enslaving Africans involved a complex network of African and European traders. African kingdoms and merchants played a role in capturing and selling other Africans, often prisoners of war or people kidnapped from rival communities, to European traders. These captives were transported to coastal forts and trading posts, where they were held in pens or dungeons while awaiting the arrival of slave ships. The conditions in these holding areas were appalling, with captives suffering from overcrowding, disease, and abuse.

The journey of the Middle Passage began when these captives were loaded onto slave ships bound for the Americas. The ships were designed to maximize profit, often at the expense of the captives' well-being. Men, women, and children were packed tightly into the hold of the ships, chained together and given barely enough space to sit or lie down. The captives were kept in darkness and squalor, with little ventilation, and the stench of human waste was overwhelming. The lack of sanitation and fresh air created a breeding ground for disease, and outbreaks of dysentery, smallpox, and other illnesses were common.

The duration of the Middle Passage varied depending on the point of departure and the final destination, but it typically lasted between six to eight weeks. During this time, the captives were subjected to the most brutal conditions imaginable. They were fed meager rations of food, often consisting of beans, rice, and yams, which were barely sufficient to sustain them. Freshwater was scarce, leading to dehydration. The captives were also subjected to physical abuse and violence from the crew. Whippings and beatings were common as a means of maintaining control and discipline. Women and young girls were particularly vulnerable to sexual abuse and exploitation by the crew members.

The psychological trauma of the Middle Passage was immense. Captives were torn from their homeland, separated from their families and communities, and faced the uncertainty of their fate. The experience of being shackled, confined, and dehumanized took a severe toll on their mental and emotional well-being. Many captives succumbed to despair, and suicide attempts were not uncommon. Some captives chose to jump overboard, preferring death to the horrors they faced on the ship.

Mortality rates during the Middle Passage were staggeringly high. It is estimated that between 15% to 25% of the captives did not survive the journey. This meant that out of the approximately 12.5 million

Africans who were shipped across the Atlantic, about 1.8 to 3 million perished during the voyage. The bodies of those who died were often thrown overboard, sometimes while still shackled, serving as grim reminders of the voyage's brutality.

Upon arrival in the Americas, the survivors of the Middle Passage faced a life of enslavement and further hardship. They were taken to slave markets where they were inspected, auctioned off, and sold to the highest bidder. The process of being sold was dehumanizing, as captives were treated as commodities, stripped of their identity and dignity. Families were often separated, with members being sold to different owners and scattered across vast distances.

The labor demands in the New World varied by region and crop, but the conditions for enslaved Africans were uniformly harsh. In the Caribbean and the southern United States, where sugar and cotton plantations dominated, slaves worked long hours under the blistering sun, subjected to grueling physical labor. The brutal conditions on sugar plantations, in particular, were notorious for their high mortality rates. The combination of exhausting work, inadequate nutrition, and severe punishment contributed to a life expectancy of just seven to ten years for many slaves in these regions.

The economic impact of the transatlantic slave trade was profound, contributing significantly to the wealth and development of European nations and their colonies. The labor of enslaved Africans was crucial to the production of commodities that fueled the growth of global trade and capitalism. The profits generated from the slave trade and the exploitation of slave labor were used to finance industrialization in Europe, build infrastructure, and support the rise of financial institutions.

The cultural impact of the Middle Passage and the broader transatlantic slave trade was equally significant. The forced migration and enslavement of millions of Africans led to the creation of diverse African diasporic communities in the Americas. These communities retained elements of their African heritage, including language, religion, music, and cultural practices, while also adapting to and influencing the cultures of their new environments. The rich cultural contributions of African diasporic communities have had a lasting impact on the art, music, cuisine, and social fabric of the Americas.

The legacy of the Middle Passage is one of immense suffering and resilience. The descendants of those who survived the journey and the subsequent enslavement have continued to fight for recognition, justice, and equality. The abolition of the transatlantic slave trade and slavery itself was a protracted struggle, involving resistance and rebellion by the enslaved, advocacy by abolitionists, and significant social and political upheaval. In the United States, the Civil War (1861-1865) was a pivotal conflict that led to the abolition of slavery, but the struggle for civil rights and equality continued long after.

The memory of the Middle Passage and its victims is preserved through various forms of commemoration, scholarship, and cultural expression. Memorials, museums, and educational initiatives aim to honor the lives lost and to educate future generations about the atrocities of the transatlantic slave trade. Literature, music, and art have also played a crucial role in keeping the memory of the Middle Passage alive, providing a means for the descendants of the enslaved to express their heritage, pain, and resilience.

Chapter 15: Slavery in Colonial America

Slavery in colonial America was a complex and brutal institution that profoundly shaped the social, economic, and political landscape of the colonies. The system of slavery evolved over time, becoming deeply entrenched and institutionalized. Central to this system were the plantations, which became the primary sites of labor for enslaved Africans. The conditions on these plantations were harsh, and the punishments meted out to slaves were severe and inhumane. This long and detailed exploration of slavery in colonial America will examine the development of the plantation economy, the daily lives of enslaved people, the forms of punishment used to maintain control, and the broader social and political implications of slavery.

The roots of slavery in colonial America can be traced back to the early 17th century, with the arrival of the first enslaved Africans in Jamestown, Virginia, in 1619. Initially, the labor force in the English colonies consisted of indentured servants, both European and African, who worked under contract for a fixed period in exchange for passage to the New World. However, as the demand for labor grew, especially in the southern colonies where tobacco, rice, and indigo became major cash crops, planters increasingly turned to African slaves as a more permanent and controllable labor force.

The transition from indentured servitude to chattel slavery was marked by a series of legal and social changes that codified racial distinctions and established the lifelong, inheritable status of African slaves. By the late 17th century, colonial legislatures had enacted laws that defined slavery as a condition passed from mother to child, ensuring the perpetuation of the system. These laws also stripped enslaved people of basic rights and legal protections, allowing slaveholders to exercise near-total control over their lives.

Plantations, large agricultural estates, became the epicenters of the colonial slave economy. The geography and climate of the southern colonies were well-suited to the cultivation of labor-intensive crops such as tobacco, rice, and later cotton. The plantation system required a substantial and continuous labor force, which was provided by the importation of African slaves. The transatlantic slave trade, which brought millions of Africans to the Americas, fueled the growth of the plantation economy and entrenched the institution of slavery.

The daily lives of enslaved people on plantations were characterized by relentless labor, harsh living conditions, and constant surveillance. From sunrise to sunset, enslaved men, women, and children were forced to work in the fields, performing tasks such as planting, tending, and harvesting crops. The work was physically demanding and exhausting, often carried out under the scorching sun or in treacherous conditions such as swamps and rice paddies.

In addition to fieldwork, enslaved people were also tasked with a variety of other duties, including maintaining the plantation infrastructure, caring for livestock, and performing skilled labor such as blacksmithing, carpentry, and weaving. Inside the plantation households, enslaved domestic workers cooked, cleaned, and cared for the slaveholders' families. Regardless of their specific roles, all enslaved people were subject to the whims and demands of their owners.

The living conditions for enslaved people were deplorable. They were typically housed in crude cabins made of wood or mud, with dirt floors and little protection from the elements. These cabins were overcrowded, poorly ventilated, and lacked basic sanitation. Enslaved people received minimal rations of food, often consisting of cornmeal, pork, and other low-quality provisions. Malnutrition and poor health were common, exacerbated by the grueling labor and lack of medical care.

The plantation system relied on a regime of surveillance and punishment to maintain control over the enslaved population. Slaveholders employed various methods to instill fear and obedience, including physical violence, psychological intimidation, and social manipulation. Punishments for perceived infractions or acts of resistance were severe and designed to deter others from challenging the authority of the slaveholder.

Physical punishment was the most immediate and visible form of control. Whipping was the most common method, used to discipline enslaved people for a wide range of offenses, from failing to meet work quotas to acts of defiance. Enslaved people were often whipped in public as a means of humiliating them and reinforcing the power dynamics on the plantation. Other forms of corporal punishment included branding, mutilation, and confinement in stocks or other devices.

In addition to physical punishment, slaveholders employed psychological tactics to break the spirit of the enslaved. They manipulated social relationships by separating families, selling individuals to distant locations, and fostering mistrust among the enslaved community. The constant threat of violence and the uncertainty of their fate created an environment of pervasive fear and anxiety.

Despite the harsh conditions and relentless oppression, enslaved people found ways to resist and assert their humanity. Resistance took many forms, from subtle acts of defiance to organized revolts. Enslaved people slowed down their work, sabotaged equipment, feigned illness, and maintained their cultural traditions as forms of everyday resistance. Some managed to escape, seeking refuge in maroon communities, Native American territories, or the northern colonies where slavery was less entrenched.

There were also more overt acts of resistance, including rebellions and insurrections. Notable examples include the Stono Rebellion in South Carolina in 1739, where a group of enslaved Africans armed themselves and attempted to march to Spanish Florida, where they had been promised freedom. Although the rebellion was ultimately suppressed, it demonstrated the courage and determination of enslaved people to fight for their liberty.

The fear of slave uprisings was a constant concern for slaveholders and colonial authorities, leading to the implementation of strict slave codes that further curtailed the freedoms of enslaved people and imposed harsh penalties for resistance. These laws prohibited enslaved people from learning to read and write, restricted their movement, and imposed curfews. They also granted slaveholders the legal right to use lethal force to suppress resistance.

The economic impact of slavery on colonial America was significant. The wealth generated by the labor of enslaved people fueled the growth of the colonial economy, particularly in the southern colonies. The profits from cash crops such as tobacco, rice, and indigo were reinvested in land, slaves, and infrastructure, creating a cycle of wealth accumulation that benefited a small elite of slaveholders. This economic system created stark disparities in wealth and power, entrenching a rigid class hierarchy that persisted long after the abolition of slavery.

The political implications of slavery were equally profound. The institution of slavery shaped the development of colonial laws and governance, influencing the creation of legal and political structures that perpetuated racial inequality. The presence of a large enslaved population also affected the balance of power between the colonies and the British Crown, as colonial elites sought to maintain control over their labor force and resist interference from external authorities.

The ideological justification for slavery was rooted in a combination of economic interests, racial theories, and religious beliefs. Slaveholders and their supporters argued that slavery was necessary for the economic prosperity of the colonies and that Africans were naturally suited for enslavement due to their perceived racial inferiority. These beliefs were reinforced by pseudoscientific theories and interpretations of biblical texts that were used to legitimize the dehumanization of enslaved people.

The American Revolution (1775-1783) brought the contradictions of slavery into sharp relief. The rhetoric of liberty and equality espoused by the American colonists stood in stark contrast to the reality of slavery. Some revolutionary leaders, including Thomas Jefferson and George Washington, were themselves slaveholders, grappling with the tension between their ideals and their economic interests. The Revolution sparked debates about the morality of slavery, leading to gradual emancipation in some northern states and heightened tensions over the future of slavery in the new nation.

In the decades following the Revolution, the institution of slavery became even more entrenched in the southern United States, particularly with the invention of the cotton gin in 1793. This technological innovation made the cultivation of cotton highly profitable, leading to the expansion of the plantation system and an increased demand for enslaved labor. The domestic slave trade grew, with thousands of enslaved people being forcibly relocated to the Deep South to work on cotton plantations.

The growing divide between the northern and southern states over the issue of slavery set the stage for the Civil War (1861-1865). The war was a pivotal moment in American history, culminating in the abolition of slavery with the passage of the 13th Amendment in 1865. However, the legacy of slavery continued to shape American society, as formerly enslaved people faced significant challenges in their pursuit of freedom and equality.

Reconstruction (1865-1877) was a turbulent period marked by efforts to integrate formerly enslaved people into American society and grant them civil rights. Despite some progress, including the passage of the 14th and 15th Amendments, which granted citizenship and voting rights to African Americans, the period was also characterized by violent resistance from white supremacists and the establishment of Jim Crow laws that enforced racial segregation and disenfranchisement.

The legacy of slavery has had a lasting impact on American society, contributing to systemic racial inequalities that persist to this day. The economic, social, and political structures established during the colonial period laid the foundation for enduring disparities in wealth, education, and opportunity. The struggle for civil rights and social justice continues, as descendants of enslaved people seek to address the historical injustices and build a more equitable society.

Chapter 16: Revolt and Resistance: Slave Rebellions

Slave rebellions and resistance movements were vital components of the history of slavery, reflecting the relentless struggle of enslaved individuals to reclaim their freedom and humanity. These acts of defiance, ranging from subtle forms of resistance to large-scale revolts, were a testament to the indomitable spirit and resilience of those who endured the brutal conditions of slavery. This detailed examination of slave rebellions will explore the various forms of resistance, notable uprisings, and their profound impact on the institution of slavery and the broader society.

Enslaved people employed a wide array of resistance strategies to undermine the institution of slavery and assert their agency. Resistance could be covert or overt, individual or collective, and it took place in different contexts, including plantations, urban settings, and during transportation. Understanding the spectrum of resistance helps to appreciate the complexity and ingenuity of enslaved individuals in their fight against oppression.

Covert resistance included everyday acts of defiance that disrupted the smooth operation of the plantation system without direct confrontation. These acts ranged from work slowdowns, feigning illness, and sabotage of tools and equipment to theft and running away. Enslaved people might deliberately work at a slower pace to reduce productivity or perform tasks incorrectly to undermine the master's efforts. These subtle forms of resistance were difficult to detect and punish but cumulatively had a significant impact on the plantation economy.

Running away was a common form of resistance, with enslaved individuals seeking temporary or permanent escape from bondage. Some runaways, known as "maroons," established independent communities in remote areas, often in swamps, mountains, or forests, where they could live free from the control of slaveholders. These maroon communities existed throughout the Americas, notably in Jamaica, Suriname, and the southeastern United States. The presence of maroon communities posed a constant challenge to the slave system and sometimes led to violent confrontations between maroons and colonial authorities.

In addition to covert resistance, there were also numerous instances of overt rebellion, where enslaved people engaged in organized, armed uprisings against their oppressors. These rebellions were often driven by a combination of factors, including harsh conditions, inspiration from other successful revolts, and the hope of achieving freedom. While many revolts were suppressed with brutal force, they nonetheless had a lasting impact on the institution of slavery and the societies in which they occurred.

One of the earliest and most significant slave rebellions in the New World was the 1521 revolt in Hispaniola (modern-day Haiti and the Dominican Republic). Enslaved Africans, who had been brought to work on Spanish plantations and in mines, rose up against their masters in a bid for freedom. Although the rebellion was ultimately crushed, it set a precedent for future resistance and highlighted the determination of enslaved people to fight against their subjugation.

The Stono Rebellion of 1739 in South Carolina was another major uprising that had a profound impact on the colonial slave system. Led by a literate slave named Jemmy, a group of enslaved Africans armed themselves and marched towards Spanish Florida, where they had been promised freedom. The rebels killed several white colonists and burned plantations along the way. Although the rebellion was eventually suppressed by the colonial militia, it instilled fear in the hearts of slaveholders and led to the implementation of stricter slave codes to prevent future uprisings.

In the Caribbean, the brutal conditions on sugar plantations fueled numerous rebellions. One of the most famous was the Haitian Revolution (1791-1804), a successful slave revolt that resulted in the abolition of slavery and the establishment of the first independent black republic in the Americas. The revolution began with a massive uprising of enslaved Africans in the northern part of the French colony of Saint-Domingue. Led by figures such as Toussaint L'Ouverture, Jean-Jacques Dessalines, and Henri Christophe, the rebels fought against the French colonial forces and their allies. The Haitian Revolution was a watershed moment in the history of slavery, demonstrating that enslaved people could successfully overthrow their oppressors and achieve self-determination.

The Haitian Revolution had far-reaching consequences, inspiring enslaved people and abolitionists across the Americas and instilling fear among slaveholders. In the United States, the specter of a similar revolt loomed large, leading to increased repression and the enactment of more stringent slave codes. Despite this, resistance continued, with notable uprisings such as Gabriel's Rebellion in 1800 and Nat Turner's Rebellion in 1831.

Gabriel's Rebellion, also known as Gabriel's Conspiracy, took place in Richmond, Virginia. Gabriel, an enslaved blacksmith, planned a large-scale insurrection aimed at capturing the state capital and negotiating the end of slavery in Virginia. The conspiracy involved hundreds of enslaved and free blacks, but it was thwarted by bad weather and betrayal. Gabriel and several of his co-conspirators were captured and executed, but the rebellion heightened the anxieties of slaveholders and led to harsher restrictions on the movement and assembly of enslaved people.

Nat Turner's Rebellion in 1831 was one of the most significant and violent slave uprisings in American history. Nat Turner, a literate enslaved preacher, believed he was divinely inspired to lead his people out of bondage. Turner and his followers launched a rebellion in

Southampton County, Virginia, killing around 60 white men, women, and children. The rebellion was eventually suppressed by the state militia, and Turner was captured and executed. In the aftermath, there was widespread panic among slaveholders, leading to brutal reprisals against enslaved people and the implementation of even more repressive laws.

Slave rebellions were not limited to the English colonies and the United States. In Brazil, which had the largest population of enslaved Africans in the Americas, there were numerous uprisings. The most famous was the Malê Revolt of 1835 in Salvador, Bahia, led by Muslim African slaves. The rebels, many of whom were literate and had military experience, planned to overthrow the government and establish a Muslim state. Although the rebellion was suppressed, it highlighted the potential for organized resistance among the enslaved population and led to increased efforts to control and assimilate African cultural and religious practices.

In the British Caribbean, the Demerara Rebellion of 1823 in present-day Guyana was a major uprising that had significant implications for the abolition movement. The rebellion involved thousands of enslaved people who believed they had been granted their freedom by the British government but were being denied their rights by local planters. Led by an enslaved man named Quamina and his son Jack Gladstone, the rebels initially sought a peaceful resolution but eventually resorted to armed resistance. The rebellion was brutally suppressed, but it drew attention to the injustices of slavery and galvanized support for abolition in Britain.

The Morant Bay Rebellion of 1865 in Jamaica, though occurring after the abolition of slavery in the British Empire, was another significant uprising that reflected the ongoing struggle for freedom and justice. Led by Paul Bogle, a Baptist preacher, the rebellion was sparked by economic hardship, social inequality, and racial discrimination. The rebels attacked the Morant Bay courthouse and killed several officials.

The British response was swift and severe, with Governor Edward Eyre declaring martial law and executing hundreds of suspected rebels. The rebellion and its aftermath highlighted the enduring legacy of slavery and the continued fight for civil rights and social justice.

In addition to organized rebellions, there were also numerous instances of individual acts of resistance and heroism. Figures such as Harriet Tubman, Frederick Douglass, and Sojourner Truth emerged as leaders in the fight against slavery, using their voices and actions to challenge the institution and advocate for freedom and equality. Harriet Tubman, an escaped slave, became a conductor on the Underground Railroad, leading hundreds of enslaved people to freedom in the northern United States and Canada. Frederick Douglass, an escaped slave and prominent abolitionist, used his eloquent oratory and writing to expose the horrors of slavery and advocate for its abolition. Sojourner Truth, an escaped slave and powerful speaker, campaigned for abolition, women's rights, and social justice.

The impact of slave rebellions and resistance on the institution of slavery was profound. These acts of defiance challenged the moral and economic foundations of slavery, exposing its inherent brutality and injustice. They also demonstrated the agency and humanity of enslaved people, countering the dehumanizing narratives propagated by slaveholders and their supporters. The fear of rebellion forced slaveholders to implement increasingly repressive measures to maintain control, but it also highlighted the inherent instability and unsustainability of the slave system.

The legacy of slave rebellions continues to resonate in contemporary society. These acts of resistance are remembered and commemorated as powerful symbols of the struggle for freedom and justice. They serve as a reminder of the resilience and courage of those who fought against oppression and as a call to action in the ongoing fight against racial inequality and injustice.

Chapter 17: The Abolition Movement: Struggle for Freedom

The abolition movement was a historic and multifaceted campaign that spanned several centuries and continents, aiming to end the institution of slavery and secure freedom for millions of enslaved individuals. This movement involved a diverse coalition of activists, including enslaved people, free African Americans, white allies, religious leaders, and political figures, who employed a variety of strategies to achieve their goals. The struggle for freedom was marked by intense moral, political, and social battles, culminating in significant legislative victories that reshaped societies.

The roots of the abolition movement can be traced back to the early resistance efforts of enslaved people themselves. From the moment they were enslaved, individuals resisted through revolts, escape, and the preservation of cultural and familial bonds. These acts of defiance laid the groundwork for a more organized movement that would emerge in the 18th century.

In the early modern period, the transatlantic slave trade expanded dramatically, driven by European colonial powers and their demand for labor in the Americas. The horrific conditions of the Middle Passage, where millions of Africans were forcibly transported across the Atlantic, and the brutal realities of plantation life sparked outrage and condemnation among some Europeans and Americans. Religious groups, particularly the Quakers, played a crucial role in the early abolitionist efforts. Quakers in both Britain and the American colonies began to voice opposition to slavery as early as the late 17th century, arguing that it was incompatible with Christian principles of equality and compassion.

In the 18th century, Enlightenment ideas about human rights and the inherent dignity of individuals further fueled the abolitionist cause.

Philosophers such as John Locke and Jean-Jacques Rousseau advocated for the natural rights of man, concepts that contradicted the existence of slavery. These intellectual currents, combined with the growing humanitarian awareness, laid the ideological foundation for the abolition movement.

The abolitionist movement gained significant momentum in Britain during the late 18th century. Key figures emerged who would play pivotal roles in the struggle against slavery. Granville Sharp, a lawyer and one of the earliest British abolitionists, became involved in the cause after assisting an escaped enslaved African, Jonathan Strong, who had been beaten and left for dead by his owner. Sharp's legal efforts resulted in a landmark case in 1772, known as the Somerset Case, where the English courts ruled that slavery was not supported by English common law. This decision effectively ended the legal standing of slavery in Britain, though it did not immediately abolish the institution in the British colonies.

Another significant figure in the British abolition movement was Thomas Clarkson. In 1787, Clarkson helped found the Society for Effecting the Abolition of the Slave Trade, alongside notable abolitionists like William Wilberforce and Granville Sharp. Clarkson's efforts to gather evidence of the brutal conditions aboard slave ships and the horrors of the slave trade played a crucial role in raising public awareness and building support for the abolitionist cause.

William Wilberforce, a Member of Parliament, became the most prominent political figure in the British abolition movement. For over two decades, Wilberforce tirelessly campaigned for the abolition of the slave trade, delivering powerful speeches and introducing numerous bills in Parliament. His perseverance paid off in 1807 when the British Parliament passed the Abolition of the Slave Trade Act, which made it illegal to participate in the transatlantic slave trade. However, this legislation did not immediately end slavery within the British Empire. It would take another 26 years of persistent effort before the Slavery

Abolition Act of 1833 was passed, leading to the emancipation of enslaved people in most British colonies.

In the United States, the abolition movement faced unique challenges due to the deeply entrenched nature of slavery, particularly in the southern states. The movement gained traction in the late 18th and early 19th centuries, influenced by both religious and Enlightenment ideals. Prominent early American abolitionists included figures such as Anthony Benezet, a Quaker who founded one of the first abolitionist societies in America, and Benjamin Rush, a signer of the Declaration of Independence who advocated for the abolition of slavery on both moral and scientific grounds.

The rise of the abolitionist movement in the United States was marked by the publication of influential literature that exposed the horrors of slavery and galvanized public opinion. One of the most significant works was "Uncle Tom's Cabin" by Harriet Beecher Stowe, published in 1852. The novel's vivid depiction of the brutality of slavery and the suffering of enslaved individuals captivated readers and intensified the national debate over slavery. Stowe's work, along with other abolitionist writings, helped to humanize enslaved people and generated widespread empathy and support for the abolitionist cause.

Frederick Douglass, an escaped slave who became one of the most powerful voices in the abolition movement, used his eloquence and personal experience to advocate for the end of slavery. His autobiography, "Narrative of the Life of Frederick Douglass, an American Slave," published in 1845, provided a firsthand account of the brutality of slavery and the struggle for freedom. Douglass's speeches and writings, along with his involvement in the Underground Railroad, made him a key figure in the movement.

The Underground Railroad was a network of secret routes and safe houses that helped enslaved people escape to free states and Canada. Harriet Tubman, another escaped slave and prominent abolitionist, played a critical role in this network. Known as the "Moses of her people," Tubman made numerous trips back to the South to guide enslaved individuals to freedom, risking her life each time. Her bravery and dedication became emblematic of the broader abolitionist struggle.

Abolitionist societies and organizations proliferated during the 19th century, providing a platform for activists to coordinate efforts and share strategies. The American Anti-Slavery Society, founded in 1833 by William Lloyd Garrison, was one of the most influential abolitionist organizations in the United States. Garrison's radical approach, including his insistence on immediate emancipation and his willingness to confront pro-slavery elements directly, often put him at odds with more moderate abolitionists. Nevertheless, his publication, "The Liberator," became a crucial voice in the movement, spreading abolitionist ideas and rallying support.

Women's involvement in the abolition movement was also significant. Many women, including notable figures such as Sojourner Truth, Lucretia Mott, and the Grimké sisters, played active roles in advocating for the end of slavery. Their participation in the movement often intersected with their fight for women's rights, as they drew parallels between the oppression of enslaved individuals and the subjugation of women. The Seneca Falls Convention of 1848, a landmark event in the women's rights movement, was attended by many abolitionists, highlighting the interconnected nature of these social justice causes.

The abolition movement faced substantial opposition, particularly from those with vested economic interests in the continuation of slavery. Pro-slavery advocates employed various arguments to defend the institution, ranging from economic necessity and racial superiority to interpretations of biblical texts. The tensions between abolitionists and pro-slavery factions often erupted into violent confrontations, such as the infamous attack on abolitionist newspaper editor Elijah Lovejoy, who was killed by a pro-slavery mob in 1837.

The political landscape in the United States became increasingly polarized over the issue of slavery. The Missouri Compromise of 1820, the Compromise of 1850, and the Kansas-Nebraska Act of 1854 were all attempts to balance the interests of slave and free states, but they ultimately failed to resolve the underlying conflict. The Dred Scott decision of 1857, in which the Supreme Court ruled that African Americans could not be considered citizens and that Congress had no authority to prohibit slavery in the territories, further inflamed tensions.

The election of Abraham Lincoln as President in 1860, on a platform that opposed the expansion of slavery, was the catalyst for the secession of Southern states and the outbreak of the Civil War. The war initially aimed to preserve the Union, but it soon became a fight to end slavery. The Emancipation Proclamation, issued by Lincoln in 1863, declared the freedom of all enslaved people in Confederate-held territory. Although it did not immediately free all enslaved individuals, it fundamentally transformed the character of the war and made the abolition of slavery a central goal of the Union effort.

The eventual Union victory in the Civil War led to the passage of the 13th Amendment to the United States Constitution in 1865, which abolished slavery throughout the country. This legislative victory was the culmination of decades of relentless struggle by abolitionists and the sacrifices of countless enslaved individuals who had fought for their freedom.

The abolition of slavery in the United States had profound and far-reaching effects. It marked the end of a brutal and dehumanizing institution that had shaped the nation's social, economic, and political landscape. However, the legacy of slavery continued to influence American society, as formerly enslaved individuals faced significant challenges in their pursuit of true freedom and equality. The period of Reconstruction, which followed the Civil War, saw efforts to integrate African Americans into the political and social fabric of the nation, but these efforts were met with fierce resistance and ultimately gave way to the era of Jim Crow laws and systemic racial discrimination.

The global impact of the abolition movement extended beyond the United States and Britain. The movement inspired similar efforts in other parts of the world, contributing to the eventual abolition of slavery in places such as Brazil, Cuba, and the French colonies. The struggle for freedom and human rights that defined the abolition movement laid the groundwork for future social justice movements, including the civil rights movement of the 20th century and ongoing efforts to address racial inequality and injustice.

Chapter 18: Post-Civil War America

The end of the Civil War in 1865 marked a pivotal moment in American history, not only because it concluded the bloodiest conflict on American soil but also because it heralded the emancipation of millions of enslaved African Americans. However, the promise of freedom and equality for African Americans was far from realized with the abolition of slavery. The period following the Civil War, known as Reconstruction (1865-1877), was a tumultuous era of significant social, economic, and political change. This era saw the struggle for civil rights, the rise and fall of Reconstruction policies, the persistent resistance of white supremacy, and the eventual establishment of Jim Crow laws. The legacy of emancipation and its aftermath continued to shape American society well into the 20th century and beyond.

The Emancipation Proclamation, issued by President Abraham Lincoln on January 1, 1863, was a significant wartime measure that declared all slaves in Confederate-held territory to be free. However, it did not immediately free all enslaved individuals, particularly those in border states and areas under Union control. The true legal abolition of slavery came with the passage of the 13th Amendment to the U.S. Constitution, ratified on December 6, 1865, which abolished slavery throughout the United States. This monumental legislative achievement marked the beginning of a new chapter for African Americans, but it also presented a host of challenges and uncertainties.

The immediate aftermath of emancipation was characterized by a chaotic and often violent transition. Freedmen and freedwomen faced the daunting task of rebuilding their lives in a society that had long denied their humanity and basic rights. The federal government, recognizing the need to assist newly freed African Americans, established the Freedmen's Bureau in March 1865. This agency provided food, housing, medical aid, education, and legal assistance. It also helped to negotiate labor contracts and establish schools. Despite its noble intentions, the Freedmen's Bureau faced significant opposition from white southerners and was chronically underfunded and understaffed, limiting its effectiveness.

One of the most pressing issues in the immediate post-war period was the question of land. Many freedmen believed that they were entitled to land as compensation for their years of unpaid labor and as a means to secure their economic independence. The slogan "40 acres and a mule" became a symbol of this aspiration. General William Tecumseh Sherman's Special Field Orders No. 15, issued in January 1865, temporarily allocated land to freedmen in the Sea Islands and coastal areas of Georgia and South Carolina. However, this promise was largely unfulfilled. President Andrew Johnson, who succeeded Lincoln after his assassination in April 1865, reversed many of these land grants, returning the property to its pre-war owners. This decision forced many freedmen into exploitative labor arrangements such as sharecropping and tenant farming, which often perpetuated economic dependency and poverty.

The political landscape of post-Civil War America was marked by intense debates over the status and rights of freed African Americans. Radical Republicans in Congress, who were committed to ensuring equal rights for all citizens, clashed with President Johnson, who advocated for a lenient approach to the defeated southern states. This conflict culminated in the passage of the Reconstruction Acts of 1867, which divided the South into military districts and required states to ratify the 14th Amendment and extend voting rights to African American men before they could be readmitted to the Union.

The 14th Amendment, ratified in 1868, was a landmark in American constitutional history. It granted citizenship to all persons born or naturalized in the United States, including former slaves, and promised "equal protection of the laws." The 15th Amendment, ratified in 1870, further extended voting rights by prohibiting states from denying the right to vote based on race, color, or previous condition of servitude. These amendments represented significant strides toward equality and were crucial in laying the legal foundation for future civil rights advancements.

During Reconstruction, African Americans made remarkable political gains. For the first time, African American men were elected to local, state, and federal offices. Figures such as Hiram Revels and Blanche K. Bruce served as U.S. Senators, while numerous others held positions in state legislatures and local governments. These achievements were a testament to the resilience and determination of African Americans to participate fully in the democratic process. However, their political influence was met with fierce resistance from white supremacists who sought to maintain racial hierarchy.

The backlash against Reconstruction policies was swift and violent. White supremacist organizations, most notably the Ku Klux Klan, emerged to intimidate and terrorize African Americans and their allies. These groups used violence, including lynching, arson, and murder, to suppress African American political participation and maintain white dominance. Despite federal efforts to curb these activities through the Enforcement Acts, which aimed to protect African American voters and prosecute violent offenders, the pervasive nature of white supremacist violence made it difficult to enforce these laws effectively.

Economic challenges also plagued the post-emancipation period. The end of slavery meant a complete overhaul of the southern economy, which had been heavily reliant on slave labor. Sharecropping and tenant farming became prevalent systems, where freedmen and poor whites would work land owned by others in exchange for a share of the crops. These systems often resulted in cycles of debt and poverty, as sharecroppers frequently received inadequate compensation and were subject to exploitative contracts. The lack of economic opportunity and land ownership kept many African Americans in conditions that were little better than slavery.

Education emerged as a crucial area of focus for African Americans during Reconstruction. Freedmen and women, recognizing education as a pathway to empowerment and advancement, established schools and sought educational opportunities despite significant obstacles. The Freedmen's Bureau, along with missionary societies and African American communities, played a vital role in founding schools and colleges, such as Howard University, Fisk University, and Hampton Institute. These institutions provided African Americans with the skills and knowledge necessary to navigate and challenge a racially oppressive society.

The end of Reconstruction in 1877 marked a significant turning point. The withdrawal of federal troops from the South as part of the Compromise of 1877 led to the dismantling of many Reconstruction-era gains. Southern states quickly enacted "Jim Crow" laws, which institutionalized racial segregation and disenfranchised African Americans. These laws, upheld by the Supreme Court's decision in Plessy v. Ferguson (1896), which established the "separate but equal" doctrine, codified racial inequality and relegated African Americans to second-class citizenship.

The Jim Crow era was characterized by widespread racial discrimination and violence. African Americans were systematically denied the right to vote through mechanisms such as literacy tests, poll taxes, and grandfather clauses. Segregation permeated every aspect of life, from schools and public transportation to restaurants and restrooms. The threat of lynching loomed large, with thousands of African Americans brutally murdered by white mobs with little to no legal repercussions. Despite these oppressive conditions, African Americans continued to resist and build institutions that supported their communities.

The Great Migration, which began in the early 20th century and continued through World War II, saw millions of African Americans leave the rural South for urban areas in the North and West. This migration was driven by the search for better economic opportunities and escape from the oppressive conditions of the Jim Crow South. The influx of African Americans into northern cities transformed the cultural and social landscape, contributing to the development of vibrant communities and the flowering of the Harlem Renaissance, a cultural and intellectual movement that celebrated African American culture and artistic achievements.

The struggle for civil rights continued to gain momentum in the early 20th century. Organizations such as the National Association for the Advancement of Colored People (NAACP), founded in 1909, played a crucial role in advocating for the rights of African Americans. The NAACP focused on legal challenges to segregation and discrimination, achieving significant victories such as the Supreme Court's ruling in Brown v. Board of Education (1954), which declared segregated public schools unconstitutional.

The modern civil rights movement of the 1950s and 1960s built on the foundation laid by earlier activists. The movement, led by figures such as Martin Luther King Jr., Rosa Parks, and Malcolm X, employed a combination of legal challenges, nonviolent protest, and civil disobedience to fight for equality. Landmark legislation, including the Civil Rights Act of 1964 and the Voting Rights Act of 1965, addressed many of the injustices that had persisted since the end of Reconstruction, dismantling legal segregation and protecting voting rights.

Despite these significant advancements, the legacy of slavery and the struggles of the post-Civil War era continued to affect African American communities. Issues such as economic disparity, systemic racism, and discrimination persisted, requiring ongoing efforts to achieve true equality. The late 20th and early 21st centuries saw continued activism and the emergence of movements such as Black Lives Matter, which highlighted the ongoing challenges faced by African Americans and advocated for systemic change.

Chapter 19: Peonage and Sharecropping

Peonage and sharecropping, though evolving in different historical and geographic contexts, represent complex and pernicious systems of bondage that emerged after the formal abolition of slavery. These systems trapped millions in cycles of debt, poverty, and exploitation, perpetuating a form of servitude that was often as dehumanizing and restrictive as chattel slavery.

Peonage, or debt servitude, primarily took hold in the post-Civil War American South and the American Southwest, as well as in parts of Latin America and other regions. After the abolition of slavery in the United States, the Southern economy, heavily dependent on labor-intensive agriculture, faced a crisis. Plantation owners, stripped of their slave labor force, sought new ways to maintain their economic dominance and labor supply. Peonage became a convenient tool for this purpose. Freed African Americans and poor whites were often coerced into signing labor contracts under the guise of employment or tenancy agreements. These contracts typically involved advances for necessities like housing, food, and clothing, which workers were expected to repay through labor. However, the wages were deliberately set so low and the prices of goods so high that workers could never earn enough to settle their debts. Consequently, they became bound to the landowner, unable to leave until their debts were paid—a virtual impossibility.

In the American Southwest, peonage was deeply rooted in the Spanish colonial system and continued under Mexican rule before becoming a widespread practice in the territories that became part of the United States. Indigenous people and mestizos were often subjected to this form of bondage, where debt repayment was used as a pretext for forced labor. The legal and social structures in these regions facilitated the entrapment of workers in perpetual servitude, with local authorities frequently complicit in upholding these unjust systems.

Parallel to peonage, sharecropping became a dominant agricultural system in the postbellum South. It emerged as a compromise between white landowners who needed labor to work their lands and freed African Americans who sought autonomy and a means of subsistence. Under sharecropping arrangements, landowners provided the land, seed, tools, and other necessities, while sharecroppers supplied the labor. The harvest was divided between the sharecropper and the landowner, ostensibly as a fair division of resources and labor. However, the reality was far more exploitative. Sharecroppers often received a disproportionately small share of the crop, leaving them unable to achieve economic independence.

The systemic abuse of sharecropping was facilitated by the crop-lien system. Sharecroppers had to borrow against their expected share of the harvest to buy supplies and food, often at exorbitant interest rates set by the landowners or local merchants. This indebtedness meant that sharecroppers rarely broke even, perpetuating a cycle of poverty and dependency. Landowners manipulated the system to their advantage, ensuring that sharecroppers remained economically subservient and socially marginalized. The lack of education and legal resources for sharecroppers further entrenched their disadvantaged position.

The racial dynamics of peonage and sharecropping cannot be overlooked. Both systems disproportionately affected African Americans, reinforcing the racial hierarchy established during slavery. Laws and practices were designed to restrict the mobility and economic opportunities of black laborers. For instance, vagrancy laws criminalized unemployment, and labor contracts were enforced with harsh penalties, including imprisonment. These legal mechanisms ensured a steady supply of cheap, controllable labor for landowners.

Despite their formal end in the early 20th century, the legacy of peonage and sharecropping persisted. The Great Migration, where millions of African Americans moved to northern cities seeking better opportunities, was partly driven by the desire to escape these oppressive systems. However, the economic and social scars left by peonage and sharecropping had long-lasting effects on the African American community, contributing to ongoing disparities in wealth, education, and social mobility.

Internationally, similar systems of debt bondage have persisted in various forms. In Latin America, debt peonage was widespread on haciendas, where indigenous and mestizo workers were tied to the land through perpetual debt. In South Asia, bonded labor remains a significant issue, with millions of workers trapped in cycles of debt and forced labor in agriculture, brick kilns, and other industries.

Efforts to eradicate peonage and sharecropping have included legal reforms, economic initiatives, and social movements. The federal government's intervention in the United States, including the Civil Rights Movement, helped dismantle some of the institutional structures supporting these systems. Land reform and labor rights movements in other parts of the world have also aimed to address the injustices of debt bondage and sharecropping.

Understanding the history and mechanisms of peonage and sharecropping is crucial in recognizing how economic systems can be manipulated to sustain inequality and exploitation. These forms of bondage serve as stark reminders that the end of formal slavery did not equate to true freedom and equality for many laborers. They underscore the importance of vigilance and activism in combating contemporary forms of labor exploitation and ensuring that all individuals have the opportunity to work in conditions of dignity and fairness.

Chapter 20: Industrial Revolution

The Industrial Revolution, spanning roughly from the late 18th to the early 19th century, marked a pivotal period of transformation in human history. It ushered in an era of unprecedented technological advancement, economic growth, and societal change. However, this era of progress also bore a darker side characterized by the widespread use of child labor and factory servitude. These phenomena highlight the complexities and contradictions of the Industrial Revolution, wherein the drive for industrial and economic advancement came at the expense of human rights and dignity.

The Industrial Revolution began in Britain and quickly spread to other parts of Europe and North America. It was driven by innovations in technology, such as the steam engine, mechanized textile production, and improvements in metallurgy. These advancements led to the establishment of factories, which became the primary sites of production. Factories required a substantial and disciplined workforce, and children were seen as an ideal source of labor due to their ability to perform repetitive tasks, willingness to accept lower wages, and adaptability to the harsh working conditions.

Child labor during the Industrial Revolution was pervasive and systematic. Children as young as five or six were employed in factories, mines, and workshops. Their small size made them suitable for tasks that required nimble fingers and the ability to navigate confined spaces. For instance, in textile mills, children worked as spinners and weavers, while in coal mines, they were often used as "trappers" to open and close ventilation doors or as "hurriers" to transport coal. The conditions under which these children worked were brutal. Factory environments were typically dark, poorly ventilated, and overcrowded. Machinery was dangerous, and accidents were common. Children worked long hours, often from dawn until dusk, with minimal breaks.

The exploitation of child labor was driven by several factors. Economic necessity played a significant role. Many families, particularly those affected by the displacement of traditional agricultural livelihoods, relied on the additional income provided by their children's labor. The wages earned by children, though meager, were crucial for the survival of impoverished families. Additionally, factory owners prioritized profit over the well-being of their workers. Employing children was cost-effective, as they could be paid significantly less than adult laborers. The lack of regulatory oversight and labor laws at the time allowed factory owners to exploit child labor with impunity.

Factory servitude, which affected both children and adults, was another hallmark of the Industrial Revolution. The factory system imposed a rigorous and often dehumanizing regime on workers. Unlike the relatively autonomous work rhythms of agrarian life, factory work was dictated by the relentless pace of machinery and the demands of production schedules. Workers had to adhere to strict timetables, with little control over their working conditions. The introduction of the factory whistle signaled the beginning and end of work shifts, emphasizing the regimented nature of factory life.

Workers in factories faced harsh and hazardous conditions. The use of steam-powered machinery, while revolutionary, introduced significant risks. Machines lacked safety guards, leading to frequent injuries. The air in factories was often filled with dust, fibers, and toxic fumes, resulting in respiratory illnesses and other health issues. The long hours and physically demanding work took a toll on the workers' bodies, leading to chronic fatigue and physical deformities. Factory owners enforced strict discipline, with severe punishments for infractions such as tardiness or talking during work. These punishments included fines, beatings, and even dismissal.

The impact of child labor and factory servitude extended beyond the physical and economic realms, affecting the social and psychological well-being of workers. Children deprived of education and a normal childhood faced stunted intellectual and emotional development. The grueling work environment fostered a sense of powerlessness and alienation among workers. The social fabric of working-class communities was strained as families grappled with the relentless demands of factory life.

The exploitation of child labor and factory servitude did not go unchallenged. Social reformers, religious leaders, and early labor activists began to draw attention to the appalling conditions faced by workers. One of the earliest and most influential critics was Robert Owen, a factory owner who implemented progressive reforms at his New Lanark mills in Scotland. Owen reduced working hours, improved living conditions, and established schools for child workers, demonstrating that industrial efficiency could be compatible with humane treatment of workers.

Public awareness and outrage grew as journalists and writers exposed the harsh realities of industrial labor. Charles Dickens, in his novels "Oliver Twist" and "Hard Times," vividly depicted the suffering of child laborers and the dehumanizing effects of factory work. Reports by social investigators such as Michael Sadler and Edwin Chadwick provided empirical evidence of the widespread abuses in factories and mines. These reports galvanized public opinion and laid the groundwork for legislative action.

The first significant legislative response to child labor came with the passage of the Factory Act of 1833 in Britain. This act limited the working hours of children and required factory owners to provide some form of education. It marked the beginning of a series of reforms aimed at improving labor conditions. Subsequent acts, such as the Mines Act of 1842, which prohibited the employment of women and children in underground mines, and the Ten Hours Act of 1847, which restricted the working hours of women and children in factories, further advanced the cause of labor rights.

In the United States, the movement against child labor gained momentum in the late 19th and early 20th centuries. Activists like Florence Kelley and organizations such as the National Child Labor Committee (NCLC) campaigned tirelessly for federal regulations. Their efforts culminated in the Fair Labor Standards Act of 1938, which established minimum age requirements for employment and set maximum hours for child workers.

Despite these legislative victories, the struggle against child labor and factory servitude continued. Industrialization spread globally, and similar patterns of exploitation emerged in other regions. In many developing countries, child labor remains a pressing issue, driven by poverty, lack of access to education, and inadequate labor laws. The fight for workers' rights and the eradication of exploitative labor practices is ongoing.

The legacy of child labor and factory servitude during the Industrial Revolution serves as a powerful reminder of the human cost of economic progress. It underscores the importance of vigilance in protecting the rights and well-being of workers, particularly the most vulnerable. As we reflect on this dark chapter in industrial history, we must recognize the achievements of those who fought for labor reforms and continue to advocate for fair and humane working conditions in the modern era. The lessons learned from the Industrial Revolution inform contemporary debates on labor rights, corporate responsibility, and the ethical dimensions of economic development, highlighting the need for a balanced approach that values both innovation and human dignity.

Chapter 21: Company Towns: Modern Feudalism

Company towns emerged as a distinctive feature of industrial capitalism, particularly in the late 19th and early 20th centuries. These towns were established by industrial enterprises, such as mining companies, steel mills, and textile factories, to house their workers near the site of production. While ostensibly designed to provide convenience and improve the living standards of workers, company towns often embodied a form of modern feudalism. In these controlled environments, the company wielded significant power over every aspect of workers' lives, from their employment to their housing, education, and even their access to goods and services. This pervasive control led to a system that, while differing from traditional feudalism in its economic basis and legal structure, mirrored its hierarchical and exploitative nature.

The concept of company towns can be traced back to the industrial revolution when the rapid expansion of industries necessitated a stable and accessible labor force. In remote or newly industrialized areas, traditional housing and infrastructure were often lacking. Companies began to build housing and amenities to attract and retain workers. Notable examples of early company towns include Pullman, Illinois, established by the Pullman Company, and Lowell, Massachusetts, developed by textile manufacturers.

The Pullman Company Town, created by George Pullman in 1880, exemplifies the idealized vision of a company town. Pullman aimed to create a model community that would attract skilled workers and foster loyalty. The town featured well-constructed homes, clean streets, schools, parks, and recreational facilities. However, this utopian facade masked a more sinister reality. The Pullman Company maintained strict control over the town, owning all property and regulating many aspects of residents' lives. Rent was deducted directly from workers' paychecks, and the company had the authority to evict workers at will. Company rules prohibited independent political activity, and any attempt to unionize was met with swift repression.

Similar dynamics played out in other company towns. In mining regions such as Appalachia, coal companies established towns to house their workers close to the mines. These towns were often isolated, with the company store being the primary source of goods. Workers were paid in scrip, a form of company-issued currency that could only be used at the company store, ensuring that wages flowed back into the company's coffers. Prices at the company store were often inflated, leaving workers perpetually in debt. This system, known as debt peonage, trapped workers in a cycle of dependence and exploitation, mirroring the serf-lord relationship of medieval feudalism.

The paternalistic control exerted by companies extended beyond economic aspects to social and cultural life. In many company towns, the company provided and controlled all public services, including schools, churches, and medical facilities. Educational curricula were often tailored to meet the company's needs, emphasizing obedience and technical skills over critical thinking. Religious services and social activities were monitored to prevent any form of dissent or union organizing. This comprehensive control fostered a sense of dependency among workers and their families, reinforcing the hierarchical structure that placed the company at the top.

Company towns also played a significant role in shaping labor relations. The close proximity of workers and management, combined with the pervasive control exercised by the company, often led to heightened tensions and conflicts. Strikes and labor disputes in company towns were common and frequently met with violent repression. The 1894 Pullman Strike is a notable example. Sparked by wage cuts without a corresponding reduction in rent, the strike escalated into a nationwide railroad boycott, leading to federal intervention and the deaths of several strikers. The strike highlighted the inherent conflicts in company towns, where the company's dual role as employer and landlord created a profound power imbalance.

Despite their exploitative nature, company towns were not uniformly negative experiences. In some cases, workers appreciated the amenities and sense of community provided by the company. For instance, the model town of Hershey, Pennsylvania, built by the Hershey Chocolate Company, offered high-quality housing, schools, and recreational facilities. However, even in such cases, the underlying power dynamics remained skewed in favor of the company, with workers' lives and livelihoods subject to corporate control.

The decline of company towns began in the mid-20th century, driven by several factors. Economic changes, such as the shift from manufacturing to service industries, reduced the need for large, localized labor forces. The rise of labor unions and the enactment of labor laws also played a crucial role. Unions fought for workers' rights to independent housing and fair wages, challenging the economic and social control exerted by companies. Additionally, the expansion of transportation infrastructure made it easier for workers to live independently from their workplaces.

The legacy of company towns is complex. While they are often remembered for their exploitative practices, they also highlight important issues related to labor rights, corporate responsibility, and community development. The paternalistic model of company towns has largely disappeared, but the underlying dynamics of control and dependence persist in various forms. For instance, in some developing countries, multinational corporations establish self-contained compounds for their workers, providing housing and amenities but also exerting significant control over their lives.

Modern parallels can also be drawn with certain practices in the tech industry, where companies like Google and Facebook offer extensive amenities and services to their employees. While these companies do not control housing or wages in the same way as traditional company towns, they create environments where employees spend a significant portion of their lives within the corporate sphere, blurring the lines between work and personal life. This can foster a sense of dependency and limit workers' engagement with the broader community.

Reflecting on the history of company towns underscores the need for vigilance in protecting workers' rights and ensuring that economic development benefits all members of society. It highlights the importance of strong labor laws, independent unions, and regulatory oversight to prevent the concentration of power in the hands of employers. As we navigate the complexities of modern capitalism, the lessons of company towns remind us that economic progress must be balanced with social justice and human dignity.

The story of company towns is a testament to the resilience of workers and their capacity to organize and fight for better conditions. It also serves as a cautionary tale about the dangers of unchecked corporate power and the enduring relevance of the struggle for workers' rights. In examining the legacy of company towns, we are reminded that true progress involves not only technological and economic advancements but also the advancement of human rights and social equity.

Chapter 22: Indentured Servitude: Contractual Slavery

Indentured servitude, often referred to as contractual slavery, was a labor system that flourished from the 17th to the 19th centuries, predominantly in colonial America and other parts of the British Empire. It emerged as a solution to labor shortages, offering a middle ground between free labor and outright slavery. While ostensibly based on mutual agreements between laborers and employers, indentured servitude frequently devolved into a system of exploitation and coercion, mirroring many aspects of traditional slavery.

The roots of indentured servitude can be traced back to Europe, where economic hardship, overpopulation, and political instability left many people in dire straits. For the impoverished masses, the New World offered the promise of land and opportunity. However, the cost of passage across the Atlantic was prohibitively high. To address this, individuals entered into indenture contracts with merchants, shipowners, or colonial employers. Under these contracts, they agreed to work for a set number of years, typically between four and seven, in exchange for passage to the Americas, food, shelter, and, occasionally, a small plot of land or money upon completion of their term.

In the American colonies, especially in regions such as Virginia and Maryland, the demand for labor to cultivate tobacco and other cash crops was insatiable. Landowners saw indentured servants as an economical and practical solution. The system allowed them to acquire labor without the immediate capital outlay required for purchasing slaves. For their part, indentured servants hoped that the completion of their service would lead to a better life, often aspiring to become landowners themselves.

However, the reality of indentured servitude was often harsh and brutal. The voyage across the Atlantic, known as the Middle Passage, was perilous. Many servants arrived malnourished, sick, and weakened from the journey. Once in the colonies, they faced grueling labor conditions. Unlike free laborers, indentured servants had limited legal rights and protections. They were bound to their employers by legal contracts, and any attempt to escape or break their indenture was met with severe punishment, including extension of service, whipping, or imprisonment.

Indentured servants were often subjected to physical abuse and harsh living conditions. Their workdays were long and arduous, frequently exceeding the agreed-upon terms. Female servants faced the additional risk of sexual exploitation and abuse. If a female servant became pregnant, her term of service could be extended to compensate for the time lost during pregnancy and childbirth. In many ways, the treatment of indentured servants closely resembled that of slaves, with the key difference being the theoretical promise of eventual freedom.

The legal framework governing indentured servitude varied across colonies but generally favored the interests of employers. Contracts were often written in complex legal language that servants, many of whom were illiterate, could not fully understand. Courts typically sided with employers in disputes, reinforcing the power imbalance inherent in the system. Additionally, servants had limited recourse if their employers failed to uphold their end of the contract, such as providing adequate food, clothing, or land upon completion of the indenture.

The exploitation of indentured servants was not confined to the American colonies. The British Empire also transported large numbers of Irish, Scots, and other Europeans to colonies in the Caribbean, where they worked on sugar plantations under equally harsh conditions. The demand for cheap labor in these colonies fueled the expansion of the indentured servitude system, with unscrupulous recruiters, known as "crimps," often deceiving or coercing individuals into signing contracts.

Indentured servitude also intersected with the transatlantic slave trade in complex ways. In the early colonial period, African slaves and European indentured servants sometimes worked side by side. Over time, as the system of chattel slavery became more entrenched and racialized, the distinctions between indentured servitude and slavery became more pronounced. African slaves were enslaved for life and their status was hereditary, while indentured servants were theoretically bound only for a fixed term. However, the brutal treatment of indentured servants blurred these distinctions, particularly in the minds of those who endured the system.

The decline of indentured servitude in the late 17th and early 18th centuries can be attributed to several factors. The increasing availability and declining cost of African slaves provided a more permanent and controllable labor force for colonial landowners. The transatlantic slave trade became more organized and profitable, leading to a significant shift in the labor dynamics of the colonies. Additionally, the gradual improvement in economic conditions in Europe reduced the number of people willing to emigrate under indenture contracts.

Despite its decline, the legacy of indentured servitude continued to influence labor systems and social hierarchies in the Americas. Many former indentured servants, once freed, struggled to find economic stability and often ended up working as tenant farmers or wage laborers. The promises of land and prosperity that had lured them to the New World often proved illusory. Moreover, the harsh treatment and exploitation they endured contributed to the broader pattern of labor coercion and racial inequality that persisted in colonial and post-colonial societies.

Indentured servitude also left a significant cultural and demographic imprint. The influx of European indentured servants contributed to the ethnically diverse population of the American colonies. Many of the descendants of these early laborers played crucial roles in the development of American society and culture.

Additionally, the shared experience of exploitation among indentured servants and African slaves laid the groundwork for complex social and racial dynamics in the colonies.

The historiography of indentured servitude has evolved over time, with scholars increasingly recognizing its importance in the broader context of labor history and colonialism. Early historical narratives often downplayed the severity of indentured servitude, portraying it as a benign or even benevolent system. However, more recent research has highlighted the coercive and exploitative nature of the system, drawing parallels with slavery and other forms of forced labor.

In examining indentured servitude, it is essential to consider its global dimensions. Similar systems of labor exploitation existed in other parts of the world, including in Asia and Africa. For instance, the British and Dutch colonial empires utilized indentured labor from India and China in their plantations and infrastructure projects in Southeast Asia, the Caribbean, and Africa. These laborers faced conditions remarkably similar to those experienced by European indentured servants in the Americas, including long hours, harsh treatment, and limited freedoms.

The parallels between indentured servitude and contemporary forms of labor exploitation are striking. Modern-day practices such as human trafficking, bonded labor, and exploitative migrant labor share many characteristics with historical indentured servitude. Workers in these systems often find themselves trapped by debt, coercion, and legal or social constraints, highlighting the enduring relevance of the issues raised by the history of indentured servitude.

Efforts to address and eradicate modern forms of labor exploitation draw on the lessons learned from the history of indentured servitude. International organizations, governments, and advocacy groups work to strengthen labor rights, enforce anti-trafficking laws, and provide support and protection for vulnerable workers. Raising awareness about the historical and contemporary realities of labor exploitation is crucial in building a more just and equitable global economy.

Reflecting on the history of indentured servitude underscores the need for vigilance in protecting workers' rights and preventing exploitation. It highlights the importance of fair labor practices, transparent contracts, and robust legal protections for all workers, regardless of their origin or status. As we navigate the complexities of modern labor markets, the lessons of indentured servitude remind us of the fundamental human rights and dignity that must underpin any system of work.

Chapter 23: Sweatshops and Labor Exploitation

Sweatshops, synonymous with labor exploitation, have been a persistent blight on the global labor landscape, especially throughout the 20th century. Defined broadly, a sweatshop is a workplace characterized by poor working conditions, long hours, low wages, and often the violation of labor laws. The evolution of sweatshops and their continued existence underscore the complex interplay between economic globalization, industrialization, and human rights.

The origins of sweatshops can be traced back to the Industrial Revolution of the 19th century, but their most infamous proliferation occurred in the 20th century. During the early part of the century, sweatshops were prevalent in the burgeoning garment industry in the United States and Europe. Immigrant labor, particularly from Eastern Europe and Italy in the U.S., was a primary source of workers for these shops. New York City's Lower East Side became a notorious hub, with thousands of small factories crammed into tenement buildings where seamstresses and tailors toiled in cramped, poorly ventilated rooms.

One of the most tragic events underscoring the dangers of sweatshops was the Triangle Shirtwaist Factory fire in 1911. The fire resulted in the deaths of 146 garment workers, most of whom were young immigrant women. Locked exits and inadequate safety measures trapped the workers, highlighting the lethal consequences of profit-driven negligence. This disaster galvanized labor reform movements, leading to significant changes in labor laws, including improved safety standards and the establishment of the International Ladies' Garment Workers' Union (ILGWU).

Despite these early reforms, sweatshops did not disappear; instead, they adapted and persisted, especially as economic conditions and labor markets shifted. The mid-20th century saw significant changes with the rise of globalization. As multinational corporations sought to minimize production costs, they increasingly outsourced manufacturing to developing countries. This shift was driven by several factors: lower labor costs, fewer regulations, and the promise of new consumer markets.

In the post-World War II era, countries in East Asia, particularly Japan, South Korea, Taiwan, and later China, became manufacturing powerhouses. The export-oriented industrialization model adopted by these nations relied heavily on labor-intensive industries such as textiles and electronics. Sweatshops proliferated as a result, employing millions in conditions reminiscent of the worst 19th-century factories. Workers endured long hours, often exceeding 12-hour days, for meager wages under unsafe conditions.

China's rapid industrialization from the late 20th century onwards epitomized the sweatshop model. Special Economic Zones (SEZs) like Shenzhen became synonymous with massive factory complexes where thousands of workers lived in dormitories and worked on assembly lines producing goods for global markets. Investigations into these factories revealed widespread labor abuses, including forced overtime, inadequate breaks, and suppression of labor organizing. The Foxconn scandal in the 2010s, where a spate of worker suicides drew attention to the harsh conditions in factories producing electronics for companies like Apple, highlighted these issues on an international stage.

The garment industry, however, remained the most notorious for sweatshops. The global shift of textile production to countries like Bangladesh, Vietnam, and India illustrated the persistent reliance on exploited labor. Bangladesh's garment industry, employing over four million workers, became emblematic of this trend. The 2013 Rana Plaza collapse, where over 1,100 workers died, was a stark reminder of the deadly conditions in sweatshops. The building housed several garment factories producing clothing for major Western brands. The disaster exposed the severe deficiencies in building safety and the exploitative practices of subcontracting that allowed major brands to distance themselves from responsibility.

Throughout the 20th century, various efforts were made to combat sweatshop conditions. Labor unions played a critical role in advocating for workers' rights, safety standards, and fair wages. However, the power and influence of unions varied significantly across countries and industries. In many developing nations, union activity was suppressed by governments and corporations alike, fearing that labor organizing would undermine economic competitiveness.

International organizations and human rights groups also sought to address labor exploitation in sweatshops. The International Labour Organization (ILO), established in 1919, worked to set international labor standards and promote decent work conditions. Conventions on child labor, forced labor, and workplace safety were crucial in establishing a framework for labor rights. However, enforcement remained a significant challenge, particularly in countries where economic pressures and corruption undermined regulatory efforts.

Consumer activism emerged as a powerful force against sweatshop labor. Campaigns like the anti-sweatshop movement of the 1990s and 2000s targeted major brands and retailers, demanding greater transparency and ethical sourcing practices. Organizations such as the Clean Clothes Campaign and the Worker Rights Consortium pressured companies to improve labor conditions in their supply chains. Boycotts, public shaming, and advocacy for corporate social responsibility led to some improvements, such as the adoption of codes of conduct and independent factory audits.

Despite these efforts, the fundamental issues of sweatshops and labor exploitation persisted into the 21st century. The global supply chain's complexity often allowed companies to evade responsibility, as production was outsourced to multiple layers of subcontractors. This diffusion of accountability made it difficult to enforce labor standards and ensure fair treatment of workers.

Technological advancements and the rise of fast fashion exacerbated the problem. The fast fashion model, characterized by rapid production cycles and low-cost garments, placed immense pressure on manufacturers to cut costs. This often translated into exploitative labor practices, with workers bearing the brunt of the demand for cheap, quickly produced clothing. Brands like Zara, H&M, and others faced scrutiny for their reliance on sweatshop labor, despite public commitments to ethical practices.

The COVID-19 pandemic further exposed the vulnerabilities of sweatshop workers. Factory closures, order cancellations, and supply chain disruptions left millions of workers without income or social protection. The precarious nature of their employment meant that many did not receive severance pay or unemployment benefits, plunging them into deeper poverty.

Addressing the persistent issue of sweatshops requires a multifaceted approach. Strengthening labor laws and their enforcement at the national level is crucial. Governments must commit to protecting workers' rights, ensuring safe working conditions, and providing social safety nets. International cooperation is also essential, with stronger mechanisms for monitoring and enforcing labor standards across borders.

Corporate responsibility plays a significant role in combating labor exploitation. Companies must go beyond superficial commitments and genuinely integrate ethical practices into their business models. This includes ensuring transparency in their supply chains, conducting regular and independent audits, and supporting workers' rights to organize and bargain collectively. Brands must be held accountable for the conditions under which their products are made, regardless of where production occurs.

Consumer awareness and activism continue to be vital. Informed consumers can drive change by demanding ethically produced goods and supporting brands that prioritize fair labor practices. Education campaigns, advocacy, and the promotion of fair-trade initiatives help raise awareness about the human cost of cheap products.

Finally, empowering workers is fundamental to eradicating sweatshops. Supporting labor unions, grassroots organizations, and worker cooperatives enables workers to advocate for their rights and negotiate better conditions. Education and training programs can also help workers acquire new skills and improve their economic prospects.

Chapter 24: The Rise of Labor Unions

The rise of labor unions represents one of the most significant social and economic developments of the last two centuries, fundamentally transforming the relationship between workers and employers. Labor unions, which are organized associations of workers formed to protect and advance their rights and interests, have played a critical role in improving working conditions, securing better wages, and advocating for social justice. Their history is a testament to the enduring struggle for workers' rights, and understanding this history provides valuable insights into the ongoing challenges faced by labor movements today.

The origins of labor unions can be traced back to the late 18th and early 19th centuries, during the Industrial Revolution. The rapid industrialization of this period brought profound changes to the workforce. Factories, mines, and mills proliferated, drawing millions of people from rural areas into urban centers in search of work. However, the conditions in these new workplaces were often harsh and exploitative. Workers faced long hours, low wages, dangerous environments, and little job security. Child labor was common, and workers had few legal protections.

In response to these conditions, workers began to organize themselves into unions. Early labor unions faced significant opposition from employers and governments. In many countries, laws prohibited workers from forming unions or going on strike. Despite these obstacles, workers persisted, driven by the need to improve their living and working conditions. One of the earliest examples of organized labor activity was the formation of trade unions in Britain, such as the Friendly Societies and the Grand National Consolidated Trades Union, which sought to unite workers from various trades in a common cause.

In the United States, the labor movement gained momentum in the mid-19th century with the establishment of the National Labor

Union (NLU) in 1866. The NLU aimed to bring together different labor organizations to fight for common goals, such as the eight-hour workday, better wages, and improved working conditions. Although the NLU dissolved in the 1870s, it laid the groundwork for future labor organizations. The Knights of Labor, founded in 1869, became one of the most influential labor unions of the late 19th century. Unlike earlier unions that focused on specific trades, the Knights of Labor sought to organize all workers, regardless of skill level, gender, or race. Their inclusive approach and broad reform agenda attracted a large membership and helped to popularize the labor movement.

One of the pivotal moments in the history of labor unions was the Haymarket Affair of 1886. The incident began as a peaceful rally in support of workers striking for an eight-hour workday in Chicago but turned violent when a bomb was thrown at police, resulting in the deaths of several police officers and civilians. The ensuing crackdown on labor activists and the trial and execution of several anarchists drew international attention to the plight of workers and the harsh responses they faced. Despite the immediate backlash, the Haymarket Affair galvanized the labor movement and is commemorated annually on May Day, or International Workers' Day.

The late 19th and early 20th centuries saw the rise of more specialized and powerful labor unions, such as the American Federation of Labor (AFL) in the United States. Founded in 1886 by Samuel Gompers, the AFL focused on organizing skilled workers into craft unions and advocating for practical, incremental improvements in wages, hours, and working conditions. The AFL's pragmatic approach and emphasis on collective bargaining made it one of the most successful labor organizations of its time.

In Europe, labor unions also gained strength and influence during this period. In Britain, the Trades Union Congress (TUC), founded in 1868, became the national federation of trade unions, coordinating labor activities and advocating for workers' rights. Similarly, in

Germany, the General German Trade Union Federation (ADGB) played a crucial role in the labor movement, advocating for social reforms and workers' protections.

The early 20th century was marked by significant labor struggles and achievements. The Triangle Shirtwaist Factory fire in 1911, which claimed the lives of 146 garment workers, highlighted the dire need for improved safety standards and labor protections. In the aftermath of the tragedy, labor unions and progressive reformers pushed for stricter regulations, resulting in substantial legislative changes. The establishment of the International Labour Organization (ILO) in 1919 further advanced the cause of workers' rights on a global scale. The ILO, a specialized agency of the United Nations, sought to promote social justice and set international labor standards, addressing issues such as child labor, forced labor, and fair wages.

The Great Depression of the 1930s profoundly impacted the labor movement, particularly in the United States. As unemployment soared and economic hardship spread, workers became increasingly militant in their demands for better conditions and job security. The passage of the National Industrial Recovery Act (NIRA) in 1933 and the Wagner Act (National Labor Relations Act) in 1935 marked significant victories for labor unions. The Wagner Act guaranteed workers the right to form unions and engage in collective bargaining, established the National Labor Relations Board (NLRB) to oversee labor disputes, and prohibited unfair labor practices by employers. These legislative achievements led to a surge in union membership and strengthened the labor movement.

The mid-20th century is often regarded as the golden age of labor unions in many industrialized countries. Union membership reached its peak, and labor unions wielded considerable political and economic influence. In the United States, the Congress of Industrial Organizations (CIO), formed in 1935, successfully organized industrial workers in key sectors such as automotive, steel, and mining.

The AFL and CIO merged in 1955, creating the AFL-CIO, a powerful federation representing millions of workers. In Western Europe, labor unions played a central role in shaping post-war reconstruction and the development of social welfare states. In countries like Sweden, Germany, and the United Kingdom, unions were instrumental in negotiating comprehensive labor protections, health care, pensions, and other social benefits.

However, the latter part of the 20th century brought significant challenges to the labor movement. The rise of globalization, deindustrialization, and the shift towards a service-based economy resulted in a decline in union membership and influence. Manufacturing jobs, which had been the stronghold of labor unions, moved to countries with lower labor costs, leading to job losses and weakened bargaining power in traditional union strongholds. The decline of heavy industry and the growth of precarious employment, such as part-time, temporary, and gig work, further eroded union membership.

In addition to economic changes, political and ideological shifts also impacted labor unions. The rise of neoliberal economic policies in the 1980s and 1990s, championed by leaders like Ronald Reagan in the United States and Margaret Thatcher in the United Kingdom, emphasized deregulation, privatization, and the reduction of union power. Anti-union legislation, such as the Taft-Hartley Act in the U.S., imposed restrictions on union activities and made it more difficult for workers to organize and strike.

Despite these challenges, labor unions continued to adapt and evolve. In response to globalization, unions began to build transnational alliances and advocate for global labor standards. Organizations like the International Trade Union Confederation (ITUC), founded in 2006, work to coordinate labor activities across borders and promote workers' rights in the global economy. The rise of social movements and coalitions, such as the Fight for $15 campaign in the United States, highlights the ongoing relevance of labor activism in addressing issues like minimum wage, income inequality, and workers' rights in the service economy.

The 21st century has also seen a resurgence of interest in labor organizing in new sectors, particularly among young workers and those in the tech industry. The rise of gig economy platforms like Uber, Lyft, and Deliveroo has sparked debates about worker classification, labor rights, and the need for new forms of unionization. Efforts to organize gig workers, tech employees, and other precarious laborers demonstrate the enduring relevance of labor unions in advocating for fair treatment and equitable working conditions.

Moreover, labor unions have increasingly recognized the importance of inclusivity and diversity within their ranks. Historically marginalized groups, including women, people of color, and immigrants, have become more prominent in union leadership and organizing efforts. The focus on intersectionality and social justice has broadened the scope of labor activism, addressing issues such as workplace discrimination, sexual harassment, and economic inequality.

Environmental sustainability has also become a key concern for modern labor unions. The concept of a "just transition" emphasizes the need to protect workers' rights and livelihoods as economies shift towards renewable energy and green technologies. Unions advocate for policies that ensure fair wages, retraining programs, and job opportunities in sustainable industries, highlighting the interconnectedness of labor rights and environmental justice.

Chapter 25: The Gig Economy: Precarious Employment

The gig economy represents a significant transformation in the nature of work, characterized by short-term contracts, freelance work, and on-demand tasks rather than traditional, long-term employment relationships. The rise of the gig economy has introduced new levels of flexibility and autonomy for some workers but has also brought substantial challenges, particularly around job security, benefits, and workers' rights. Understanding the intricacies of the gig economy requires a deep dive into its origins, growth, implications for workers, regulatory challenges, and the future of labor in this rapidly evolving landscape.

The gig economy's roots can be traced back to the broader trends of economic globalization, technological advancements, and shifts in corporate practices. The late 20th century saw significant changes in the labor market, driven by the rise of information technology and the internet. These developments facilitated the emergence of platforms that could connect workers with short-term jobs on a scale previously unimaginable. Early examples included freelance marketplaces like Elance and oDesk, which later merged to form Upwork, a leading platform for freelance work. These platforms allowed businesses to access a global pool of talent for various tasks, from graphic design to software development.

The 2008 financial crisis accelerated the gig economy's growth. As traditional employment opportunities became scarcer, both workers and employers sought more flexible and cost-effective arrangements. For workers, the gig economy offered a way to earn income in a challenging job market. For employers, it provided a means to reduce labor costs and increase flexibility by hiring workers on an as-needed basis without the long-term commitments associated with full-time employees.

The gig economy gained further momentum with the advent of mobile technology and the proliferation of smartphones. This technological shift enabled the development of on-demand service platforms, such as Uber and Lyft in the ride-sharing sector, and TaskRabbit for various household tasks. These platforms capitalized on the convenience of mobile apps to connect consumers with gig workers quickly and efficiently. Uber, founded in 2009, became one of the most prominent examples of the gig economy, revolutionizing the transportation industry by offering a flexible work model where drivers could set their schedules.

The gig economy encompasses a wide range of activities, from high-skilled freelance work to low-skilled manual labor. Freelancers in fields like writing, graphic design, and software development often enjoy greater autonomy and higher earnings potential. In contrast, workers in on-demand service sectors, such as ride-sharing, food delivery, and household tasks, typically face more precarious conditions, including lower wages, inconsistent work hours, and a lack of benefits.

One of the central issues in the gig economy is the classification of workers. Most gig workers are classified as independent contractors rather than employees. This classification has significant implications for their rights and benefits. Independent contractors are not entitled to the same protections and benefits as employees, such as minimum wage guarantees, overtime pay, health insurance, paid leave, and unemployment benefits. While this arrangement provides flexibility for both workers and employers, it also places a greater burden on workers to manage their financial and health security.

The classification of gig workers as independent contractors has sparked widespread debate and legal challenges. Critics argue that gig companies exploit this classification to avoid providing benefits and protections, effectively creating a new form of labor exploitation. High-profile lawsuits and legislative efforts have sought to reclassify gig workers as employees to ensure they receive appropriate benefits and protections. For example, in California, Assembly Bill 5 (AB5) was passed in 2019, aiming to reclassify many gig workers as employees. However, the law faced significant opposition from gig companies, leading to the passage of Proposition 22 in 2020, which exempted ride-sharing and delivery companies from AB5, allowing them to continue classifying their drivers as independent contractors.

The precarious nature of gig work extends beyond the lack of benefits. Gig workers often face income instability due to the fluctuating availability of work and the variability in demand for services. Unlike traditional employees who receive regular paychecks, gig workers' income can vary widely from week to week, making it difficult to budget and plan for the future. This income volatility is compounded by the fact that gig workers are responsible for their expenses, such as vehicle maintenance for ride-sharing drivers or equipment costs for freelance contractors.

Another significant issue is the lack of bargaining power and representation for gig workers. Traditional labor unions have struggled to organize gig workers due to the dispersed and individualized nature of gig work. Without collective bargaining, gig workers have limited ability to negotiate better pay or working conditions. Some gig workers have turned to grassroots organizing and advocacy groups to push for improvements, but these efforts face significant challenges in the face of powerful gig companies and a fragmented workforce.

The impact of the gig economy on workers' mental and physical health is also a growing concern. The pressure to constantly find and complete gigs can lead to stress and burnout. Gig workers often work long hours to make ends meet, which can result in physical exhaustion and health issues. The lack of employer-provided health insurance further exacerbates these problems, as gig workers may delay seeking medical care due to cost concerns.

Despite these challenges, the gig economy also offers potential benefits. For some workers, the flexibility to choose when and where they work is highly valuable. This flexibility can be particularly beneficial for those with caregiving responsibilities, students, or individuals seeking supplementary income. Additionally, the gig economy can provide opportunities for entrepreneurial endeavors, allowing individuals to build their businesses and pursue diverse income streams.

The global nature of the gig economy has also opened up new opportunities for workers in developing countries. Platforms like Upwork and Fiverr enable skilled workers from countries with limited local job opportunities to access global markets and earn higher incomes. However, this globalization of labor also raises concerns about wage disparities and the potential for exploitation of workers in regions with weaker labor protections.

Regulating the gig economy poses significant challenges for policymakers. Striking a balance between protecting workers' rights and preserving the flexibility that makes gig work attractive is complex. Some countries have introduced innovative regulatory approaches to address these issues. For example, in the United Kingdom, the Supreme Court ruled in 2021 that Uber drivers are workers entitled to benefits like minimum wage and holiday pay, rather than independent contractors. This ruling set a precedent for other gig economy cases and prompted discussions about the need for new labor laws to address the unique characteristics of gig work.

In the European Union, the proposed Directive on Improving Working Conditions in Platform Work aims to ensure fair working conditions, rights, and social protection for gig workers across member states. The directive includes measures to improve transparency in algorithmic management, ensure fair pay, and provide access to social security benefits. These regulatory efforts reflect a growing recognition of the need to adapt labor laws to the realities of the gig economy.

In the United States, discussions about gig economy regulation continue at the federal and state levels. The Protecting the Right to Organize (PRO) Act, passed by the House of Representatives in 2021, seeks to strengthen workers' rights to organize and collectively bargain, including provisions that could impact gig workers. However, the bill faces significant political hurdles in the Senate.

As the gig economy evolves, new models of worker organization and support are emerging. Digital labor platforms and cooperatives are exploring ways to provide gig workers with benefits and protections typically associated with traditional employment. For example, the Freelancers Union offers health insurance and other benefits to its members, addressing some of the gaps in the gig economy. Worker cooperatives, where gig workers collectively own and manage the platform, are another innovative approach to ensuring fair treatment and equitable distribution of profits.

Technology also plays a crucial role in shaping the future of the gig economy. Advances in artificial intelligence and machine learning are changing how work is assigned and managed on gig platforms. Algorithmic management, where algorithms make decisions about work allocation, performance evaluation, and compensation, raises new ethical and regulatory questions. Ensuring transparency and fairness in these systems is essential to protect gig workers from bias and exploitation.

The COVID-19 pandemic further highlighted the vulnerabilities and importance of gig workers. During the pandemic, gig workers played a vital role in delivering essential services, such as food delivery and transportation. However, they also faced increased health risks and economic instability. The pandemic underscored the need for stronger protections and support for gig workers, prompting calls for policy changes and greater recognition of their contributions.

Chapter 26: Modern-Day Slavery: Human Trafficking Today

Modern-day slavery, particularly human trafficking, represents one of the gravest human rights abuses in our contemporary world. Despite the abolition of legal slavery over a century ago, millions of individuals globally are still trapped in conditions of forced labor, sexual exploitation, and other forms of coercion.

Human trafficking is defined as the recruitment, transportation, transfer, harboring, or receipt of persons through force, fraud, or coercion, for the purpose of exploitation. This exploitation can take various forms, including forced labor, sexual exploitation, domestic servitude, forced marriage, and the removal of organs. The International Labour Organization (ILO) estimates that nearly 25 million people are victims of forced labor globally, with women and children being disproportionately affected.

The root causes of human trafficking are deeply intertwined with social, economic, and political factors. Poverty is a significant driver, as individuals in impoverished communities are more vulnerable to traffickers' promises of employment, education, or a better life. Economic disparities between and within countries create conditions where desperate individuals are willing to take risks that expose them to exploitation.

Conflict and political instability also contribute to the prevalence of human trafficking. War-torn regions and areas experiencing political unrest often see a breakdown in law and order, making it easier for traffickers to operate. Refugees and internally displaced persons (IDPs) are particularly vulnerable, as they may lack documentation, resources, and safe means of migration, making them easy targets for traffickers.

Additionally, systemic discrimination and social marginalization play critical roles. Ethnic minorities, migrant workers, and other marginalized groups often lack legal protections and social support, increasing their vulnerability to trafficking. In many cases, traffickers exploit these vulnerabilities, using manipulation and coercion to control their victims.

Human trafficking operates through complex networks that can be both highly organized and opportunistic. Organized criminal groups often run extensive trafficking operations, exploiting weaknesses in border controls, law enforcement, and legal systems. These networks are adept at exploiting loopholes in immigration laws and often have the resources to bribe officials, ensuring their activities go unchecked.

Trafficking can also be more localized and opportunistic, with smaller groups or individuals exploiting vulnerable people in their communities. In many cases, traffickers use psychological manipulation, threats of violence, and actual physical harm to control their victims. They may confiscate identification documents, threaten to harm family members, or use debt bondage, where victims are forced to work to repay a never-ending, artificially inflated debt.

Sex trafficking is one of the most pervasive forms of human trafficking. Victims are coerced into prostitution or other forms of sexual exploitation, often under the threat of violence or actual physical harm. Women and girls are the primary victims, though men and boys are also affected. Traffickers may use physical force, deception, or emotional manipulation to entrap their victims, who are then subjected to repeated exploitation and abuse.

Labor trafficking involves the forced exploitation of individuals in various industries, including agriculture, construction, manufacturing, and domestic work. Victims of labor trafficking are often subjected to grueling work conditions, long hours, little or no pay, and physical and psychological abuse. Migrant workers are particularly vulnerable, as they may be working in unfamiliar environments, lack legal status, and be unaware of their rights.

Domestic servitude is another significant form of human trafficking. Victims, often women and children, are forced to work in private homes, performing household chores and caregiving tasks under conditions of coercion and abuse. They are frequently isolated, with limited freedom of movement and communication, making it difficult for them to seek help or escape.

Child trafficking is a particularly heinous crime, involving the exploitation of children for labor, sexual exploitation, illegal adoption, or involvement in armed conflicts. Children are often trafficked for begging, petty theft, or as child soldiers in conflict zones. The psychological and physical trauma inflicted on child victims has long-lasting, devastating effects on their development and future prospects.

The global response to human trafficking involves a combination of international, regional, and national efforts. International frameworks, such as the United Nations Protocol to Prevent, Suppress and Punish Trafficking in Persons, Especially Women and Children (also known as the Palermo Protocol), provide a comprehensive approach to combating trafficking. The Palermo Protocol, adopted in 2000, establishes measures for the prevention of trafficking, the protection of victims, and the prosecution of traffickers.

The ILO's conventions, particularly Convention No. 29 on Forced Labor and Convention No. 182 on the Worst Forms of Child Labor, also play crucial roles in setting international labor standards and guiding national policies to eliminate forced labor and child exploitation. These conventions underscore the importance of addressing the root causes of trafficking and ensuring that victims receive adequate protection and support.

Regional organizations, such as the European Union, the African Union, and the Organization of American States, have also developed frameworks and initiatives to combat human trafficking. These efforts often involve enhancing cross-border cooperation, harmonizing legal standards, and providing technical assistance to member states in implementing anti-trafficking measures.

National governments are at the forefront of the fight against human trafficking, implementing laws, policies, and programs to prevent trafficking, prosecute offenders, and protect victims. Many countries have established specialized anti-trafficking units within law enforcement agencies and have enacted comprehensive anti-trafficking legislation. These measures include criminalizing all forms of trafficking, providing victim support services, and conducting public awareness campaigns to educate communities about the dangers of trafficking.

Non-governmental organizations (NGOs) play an indispensable role in combating human trafficking. They provide critical services to victims, including shelter, legal assistance, medical care, and psychological support. NGOs also engage in advocacy and public education efforts to raise awareness about trafficking and influence policy changes. Collaboration between NGOs, governments, and international organizations is essential to creating a comprehensive and effective response to trafficking.

Despite significant progress in combating human trafficking, numerous challenges remain. One of the most pressing issues is the identification and protection of victims. Trafficking victims often remain hidden due to fear, isolation, and manipulation by traffickers. Law enforcement and service providers may lack the training and resources to identify victims and provide appropriate support. Consequently, many victims go unrecognized and unassisted, perpetuating their exploitation.

The prosecution of traffickers presents another significant challenge. Human trafficking cases are complex and require substantial evidence to secure convictions. Victims may be reluctant to testify due to fear of retaliation or mistrust of authorities. Additionally, corruption within law enforcement and judicial systems can hinder the effective prosecution of traffickers. Strengthening legal frameworks, improving investigative techniques, and ensuring the protection and support of victims who testify are crucial steps in enhancing the prosecution of traffickers.

Addressing the root causes of trafficking is fundamental to preventing it. Efforts to reduce poverty, improve education, and promote economic opportunities are essential in decreasing vulnerability to trafficking. Empowering women and marginalized communities, strengthening social safety nets, and promoting safe migration practices can also mitigate the risks of trafficking. Prevention efforts must be comprehensive and address the social, economic, and political factors that contribute to trafficking.

Technological advancements present both opportunities and challenges in the fight against human trafficking. On the one hand, traffickers increasingly use digital platforms to recruit, exploit, and control victims. Online advertisements, social media, and encrypted communications facilitate the trafficking of individuals and complicate efforts to track and dismantle trafficking networks. On the other hand, technology can also be leveraged to combat trafficking. Data analytics, artificial intelligence, and digital forensics can enhance the identification of trafficking patterns, support investigations, and improve the efficiency of victim outreach and support services.

Collaboration and coordination among stakeholders are critical to addressing human trafficking effectively. Governments, international organizations, NGOs, the private sector, and communities must work together to develop and implement comprehensive strategies. Public-private partnerships can play a pivotal role in combating trafficking, particularly in sectors such as technology, finance, and transportation. Businesses have a responsibility to ensure that their supply chains are free from forced labor and to take proactive measures to prevent trafficking.

Raising public awareness about human trafficking is essential for prevention and victim identification. Public education campaigns can inform communities about the signs of trafficking, the risks associated with certain employment offers, and the resources available for victims. Engaging the media, educational institutions, and community organizations in these efforts can amplify the message and increase the reach and impact of awareness initiatives.

Supporting and empowering survivors of trafficking is crucial for their recovery and reintegration. Comprehensive support services, including medical care, psychological counseling, legal assistance, and vocational training, are essential for helping survivors rebuild their lives. Survivor-centered approaches that prioritize the dignity, autonomy, and rights of survivors are fundamental in providing effective support. Involving survivors in the development and implementation of anti-trafficking policies and programs ensures that their voices and experiences inform and guide efforts to combat trafficking.

Chapter 27: Surveillance and Control

Surveillance and control in the modern workplace have evolved significantly, leading to what can be described as the "Panopticon Workplace." This concept is rooted in the idea of the Panopticon, a theoretical prison design proposed by the English philosopher and social theorist Jeremy Bentham in the late 18th century. Bentham's Panopticon was an architectural model designed to allow a single guard to observe all prisoners without the prisoners being able to tell whether or not they were being watched. This design created a sense of constant surveillance, encouraging self-regulation among the inmates. The Panopticon has since become a powerful metaphor for the ways in which modern technologies and management practices create environments of pervasive surveillance and control.

In the context of the workplace, the Panopticon metaphor is used to describe how employers use various technologies to monitor and regulate employees' behaviors, productivity, and performance. This extensive surveillance can shape employees' experiences, behaviors, and even their mental health. Understanding the dynamics of the Panopticon Workplace requires exploring its historical roots, technological advancements, implications for workers, ethical considerations, and potential future developments.

The historical roots of workplace surveillance can be traced back to the Industrial Revolution, when factory owners began to implement strict oversight to ensure productivity and discipline among workers. The introduction of time-and-motion studies by Frederick Winslow Taylor in the early 20th century marked a significant development in the scientific management of labor. Taylor's methods aimed to optimize work processes and increase efficiency through meticulous observation and measurement of workers' movements and tasks. This approach laid the groundwork for modern surveillance practices by emphasizing the importance of monitoring and controlling labor to enhance productivity.

With the advent of digital technologies in the late 20th and early 21st centuries, workplace surveillance has become increasingly sophisticated and pervasive. Employers now have access to a wide range of tools and technologies that enable them to monitor virtually every aspect of employees' work lives. These technologies include computer monitoring software, video surveillance, GPS tracking, biometric systems, and even artificial intelligence (AI) and machine learning algorithms.

Computer monitoring software allows employers to track employees' activities on their computers, including the websites they visit, the applications they use, and the amount of time they spend on different tasks. Keylogging software can record every keystroke made by an employee, providing detailed information about their communications and work habits. Email monitoring tools can scan and analyze employees' emails for keywords, sentiments, and potential policy violations. These tools can be used to ensure compliance with company policies, protect sensitive information, and measure productivity.

Video surveillance is another common form of workplace monitoring. Cameras can be installed in various locations within the workplace to observe employees' movements and behaviors. These cameras can be equipped with facial recognition technology, enabling employers to identify and track individuals. Video surveillance can serve multiple purposes, including security, theft prevention, and monitoring employee conduct. However, the presence of cameras can also create a sense of constant scrutiny, impacting employees' sense of privacy and autonomy.

GPS tracking technology is widely used to monitor the movements of employees, particularly those who work in transportation, delivery, or field service roles. GPS devices can be installed in company vehicles or provided as part of mobile devices to track employees' locations, routes, and time spent at different job sites. This data can be used to optimize logistics, ensure timely deliveries, and verify that employees are following assigned routes and schedules. However, constant location tracking can also lead to concerns about privacy and the potential for misuse of the data.

Biometric systems are increasingly being adopted in workplaces to enhance security and streamline access control. These systems use unique physiological or behavioral characteristics, such as fingerprints, facial features, or voice patterns, to verify employees' identities. Biometric time clocks can be used to record employees' attendance, reducing the risk of time fraud. However, the collection and storage of biometric data raise significant privacy and security concerns, particularly regarding the potential for data breaches and misuse of sensitive information.

Artificial intelligence and machine learning algorithms are transforming workplace surveillance by enabling more advanced and automated monitoring capabilities. AI-powered tools can analyze vast amounts of data to detect patterns, anomalies, and potential policy violations. For example, AI can be used to monitor employees' communications for signs of insider threats, identify unusual patterns of behavior that may indicate misconduct, or assess employees' performance based on predefined metrics. While these technologies can enhance security and efficiency, they also raise ethical questions about the fairness, accuracy, and transparency of algorithmic decision-making.

The implications of the Panopticon Workplace for employees are profound and multifaceted. On one hand, surveillance can enhance productivity, security, and compliance, benefiting both employers and employees. On the other hand, pervasive monitoring can create a sense of constant scrutiny, leading to stress, anxiety, and reduced job satisfaction. The knowledge that one's actions are constantly being observed and evaluated can lead to self-censorship and conformity, stifling creativity and innovation.

One of the most significant impacts of workplace surveillance is on employees' privacy. The collection of extensive data about employees' activities, communications, and behaviors raises concerns about how this information is used, who has access to it, and how it is protected. Employees may feel that their personal boundaries are being invaded, particularly if surveillance extends beyond work-related activities to include personal communications or movements outside of work hours.

The psychological effects of constant surveillance can also be detrimental. Research has shown that employees who perceive high levels of monitoring may experience increased stress, anxiety, and burnout. The pressure to perform under constant observation can lead to a sense of insecurity and fear of making mistakes. This environment can undermine trust between employees and employers, eroding workplace morale and cohesion.

Moreover, the Panopticon Workplace can exacerbate existing power imbalances between employers and employees. Surveillance technologies are often deployed unilaterally by employers, with little input or consent from employees. This imbalance of power can lead to abuses, such as excessive monitoring, discriminatory practices, or punitive measures based on surveillance data. Employees may feel that they have no recourse to challenge or appeal decisions made based on surveillance, further entrenching their sense of vulnerability and disempowerment.

The use of AI and algorithmic decision-making in workplace surveillance introduces additional ethical and fairness concerns. AI systems can perpetuate biases present in the data they are trained on, leading to discriminatory outcomes. For example, an AI system used to monitor employee performance may unfairly penalize certain groups of employees based on biased data or flawed algorithms. Ensuring the transparency, accountability, and fairness of AI systems is crucial to prevent such outcomes and protect employees' rights.

Addressing the challenges of the Panopticon Workplace requires a multifaceted approach that balances the benefits of surveillance with the protection of employees' rights and well-being. Several strategies can be employed to achieve this balance:

1. **Transparency and Consent**: Employers should be transparent about the use of surveillance technologies, clearly communicating what data is being collected, how it is used, and who has access to it. Obtaining employees' informed consent is essential to ensure that they are aware of and agree to the monitoring practices in place.

2. **Data Minimization and Security**: Employers should adopt data minimization principles, collecting only the data necessary for legitimate business purposes. Implementing robust data security measures is crucial to protect sensitive information from unauthorized access, breaches, or misuse.

3. **Employee Involvement and Representation**: Involving employees in discussions about surveillance practices and policies can help build trust and ensure that their perspectives and concerns are considered. Establishing mechanisms for employee representation, such as works councils or unions, can provide a platform for collective bargaining and advocacy.

4. **Fairness and Accountability in AI**: Ensuring the fairness and accountability of AI systems used in workplace surveillance is critical. Employers should conduct regular audits of AI algorithms to detect and mitigate biases, ensure transparency in decision-making processes, and provide avenues for employees to challenge or appeal decisions made by AI systems.

5. **Promoting a Positive Workplace Culture**: Employers

should foster a workplace culture that values trust, respect, and employee well-being. Surveillance practices should be implemented in a way that supports these values, rather than undermining them. Encouraging open communication, providing support for employee mental health, and recognizing employees' contributions can help mitigate the negative effects of surveillance.

6. **Regulatory Frameworks**: Governments and regulatory bodies have a crucial role to play in setting standards and guidelines for workplace surveillance. Developing comprehensive data protection laws, establishing oversight mechanisms, and enforcing compliance can help protect employees' rights and ensure responsible use of surveillance technologies.

Looking to the future, the Panopticon Workplace is likely to continue evolving as new technologies emerge and workplace dynamics shift. The increasing integration of the Internet of Things (IoT), wearable devices, and augmented reality (AR) into work environments will introduce new forms of monitoring and data collection. These technologies have the potential to enhance productivity and safety but also raise additional privacy and ethical concerns.

The rise of remote work, accelerated by the COVID-19 pandemic, has further complicated the landscape of workplace surveillance. Remote work presents unique challenges for monitoring and managing employees, leading to the adoption of new surveillance tools such as remote desktop monitoring, virtual time clocks, and productivity tracking software. Balancing the need for oversight with respect for employees' privacy and autonomy in remote work settings is an ongoing challenge.

Chapter 28: The 9 to 5 Job: Standardization of Work Hours

The concept of the "9 to 5 Job" has become synonymous with the modern working life, reflecting the standardization of work hours that has shaped the daily routines of millions of workers worldwide. This standardized work schedule, typically running from 9 a.m. to 5 p.m., Monday through Friday, has deep historical roots and far-reaching implications for individuals, organizations, and societies. To fully understand the significance of the 9 to 5 workday, it is essential to explore its origins, the factors that contributed to its establishment, its impact on workers, and the ongoing debates and transformations in work schedules in the contemporary era.

The standardization of work hours has a complex history that can be traced back to the industrial revolution in the 18th and 19th centuries. Before this period, work patterns were largely dictated by agrarian cycles and the needs of local communities. People worked according to the rhythms of nature, with no fixed schedules, and work and leisure time were often interwoven. However, the advent of industrialization brought about a fundamental shift in work patterns and organization.

With the rise of factories and mass production, employers sought to maximize efficiency and productivity. This led to the establishment of regular, fixed work hours to ensure that machinery and labor were utilized optimally. Early industrial labor conditions were harsh, with workers often toiling for 12 to 16 hours a day, six days a week, under grueling conditions. The exploitation and poor working conditions sparked labor movements and demands for shorter work hours and better labor standards.

One of the key milestones in the fight for standardized work hours was the push for the eight-hour workday. The labor movement, particularly in the United States, played a crucial role in advocating for this change. The slogan "Eight hours for work, eight hours for rest, and eight hours for what we will" encapsulated the demand for a balanced division of the day. The Haymarket Affair of 1886, a pivotal event in labor history, highlighted the struggle for the eight-hour workday and the broader fight for workers' rights.

The establishment of the eight-hour workday gained momentum in the early 20th century. In 1914, the Ford Motor Company, under the leadership of Henry Ford, made a groundbreaking decision to implement an eight-hour workday for its employees while doubling their wages. This move was driven not only by a desire to improve working conditions but also by a recognition that shorter work hours could lead to higher productivity and increased consumer purchasing power. Ford's initiative set a precedent that other companies began to follow.

The passage of labor legislation further solidified the standardization of work hours. In the United States, the Fair Labor Standards Act (FLSA) of 1938 was a landmark law that established the 40-hour workweek, mandated overtime pay for hours worked beyond 40 in a week, and set minimum wage standards. This legislation was a significant victory for workers and laid the foundation for the 9 to 5 work schedule that became the norm in many industries.

The 9 to 5 workday, while providing a more structured and predictable schedule compared to earlier industrial labor conditions, has had profound implications for workers' lives. One of the primary benefits of standardized work hours is the creation of a clear boundary between work and personal life. This separation allows employees to have dedicated time for rest, leisure, and family, contributing to a better work-life balance.

However, the 9 to 5 grind has also been criticized for its rigidity and lack of flexibility. For many workers, particularly those with caregiving responsibilities or other personal commitments, adhering to a fixed schedule can be challenging. The standard workday does not accommodate the diverse needs and lifestyles of all employees, leading to stress and difficulty in managing personal and professional responsibilities.

The commute, often an integral part of the 9 to 5 workday, adds another layer of complexity. Long commutes can significantly impact workers' well-being, reducing the time available for rest, leisure, and family. The daily rush hour can also contribute to environmental pollution and traffic congestion, raising broader societal and ecological concerns.

Moreover, the standardized workday can stifle creativity and innovation. The rigid structure of the 9 to 5 schedule does not always align with the natural rhythms and productivity patterns of individuals. Some people are more productive in the early morning or late evening, and forcing everyone to adhere to the same schedule can lead to decreased efficiency and job satisfaction.

The rise of technology and the digital age has further complicated the traditional 9 to 5 workday. The proliferation of smartphones, laptops, and internet connectivity has blurred the lines between work and personal time. Many employees find themselves responding to emails, attending virtual meetings, or completing tasks outside of regular office hours, leading to an "always-on" culture. This constant connectivity can result in burnout and negatively impact mental health.

In recent years, there has been a growing movement toward more flexible work arrangements. Flexible work schedules, remote work, and telecommuting have gained popularity as alternatives to the traditional 9 to 5 workday. These arrangements offer employees greater autonomy over their work hours and location, allowing them to better balance personal and professional responsibilities. The COVID-19 pandemic accelerated the adoption of remote work, demonstrating that many jobs can be performed effectively outside of the traditional office setting.

However, the shift toward flexible work arrangements also presents challenges. Remote work can lead to feelings of isolation and disconnection from colleagues, potentially impacting teamwork and collaboration. It also requires effective time management and self-discipline, as the boundary between work and personal life becomes more fluid. Employers must find ways to support remote workers, ensuring they have the necessary resources and maintaining a sense of community and engagement.

The debate over the future of work schedules continues to evolve. Some organizations are experimenting with alternative models, such as the four-day workweek, which aims to reduce work hours while maintaining productivity. Proponents argue that shorter workweeks can lead to improved employee well-being, increased job satisfaction, and higher productivity. However, this model may not be suitable for all industries or roles, and careful consideration is needed to ensure it meets the needs of both employers and employees.

Another emerging trend is the emphasis on outcome-based work rather than time-based work. This approach focuses on the quality and results of employees' work rather than the number of hours spent at the desk. By setting clear goals and expectations, employers can provide employees with greater flexibility in how they manage their time, fostering a results-oriented culture that values efficiency and effectiveness.

Chapter 29: The Birth of Corporate Culture

The concept of corporate culture encompasses the shared values, beliefs, behaviors, and practices that characterize an organization. The birth of corporate culture can be traced back to the rise of large corporations during the industrial revolution and the subsequent development of management theories and practices in the 20th century. This culture often emphasizes uniformity and conformity, shaping the identities and behaviors of employees to align with the goals and values of the organization. To fully understand the birth and evolution of corporate culture, it is essential to explore its historical origins, the factors that contributed to its development, the implications for workers and organizations, and the ongoing debates and transformations in corporate culture in the contemporary era.

The historical roots of corporate culture can be traced back to the industrial revolution in the 18th and 19th centuries, when large-scale factories and enterprises began to emerge. Prior to this period, work was primarily organized around small-scale, family-run businesses or guilds, where the work environment was more personal and informal. The rise of factories and mass production brought about a fundamental shift in the organization of work, leading to the need for more formalized structures and management practices.

During the industrial revolution, the focus was on maximizing efficiency and productivity. This led to the development of scientific management, also known as Taylorism, pioneered by Frederick Winslow Taylor in the early 20th century. Taylor's principles of scientific management emphasized the standardization of work processes, the division of labor, and the use of time-and-motion studies to optimize productivity. Workers were seen as interchangeable parts of a machine, and the emphasis was on creating a uniform and predictable work environment.

The rise of large corporations in the early 20th century further contributed to the development of corporate culture. Companies like General Electric, Ford, and IBM began to establish formal organizational structures, policies, and procedures to manage their growing workforce. These companies recognized the importance of creating a cohesive and uniform corporate identity to ensure consistency in operations and to build a strong brand image. This period marked the beginning of the emphasis on uniformity and conformity in corporate culture.

One of the key factors that shaped the birth of corporate culture was the need for control and coordination in large organizations. As companies grew in size and complexity, it became increasingly important to have standardized practices and procedures to ensure that all employees were working towards the same goals. This led to the development of formal management practices, including hierarchical organizational structures, standardized job roles, and clear lines of authority.

The emphasis on uniformity and conformity in corporate culture was also driven by the desire to create a strong and cohesive brand identity. Companies recognized that a consistent and recognizable corporate image was essential for building trust and loyalty among customers. This led to the development of corporate branding strategies, which included the use of logos, slogans, and other visual elements to create a unified brand image. Employees were often required to adhere to specific dress codes and behavior standards to reinforce the company's brand identity.

The birth of corporate culture was also influenced by the development of human relations theories in the mid-20th century. Pioneers like Elton Mayo and Chester Barnard emphasized the importance of social and psychological factors in the workplace, recognizing that employee satisfaction and motivation were critical for productivity and performance. This led to a shift in management practices, with a greater focus on creating a positive work environment and fostering a sense of belonging and loyalty among employees.

One of the key developments in this period was the rise of corporate paternalism, where companies took on a paternalistic role in the lives of their employees. This included providing social benefits, such as housing, healthcare, and recreational facilities, to create a sense of loyalty and commitment among employees. Companies like Ford and IBM were known for their paternalistic practices, which aimed to create a stable and motivated workforce.

The birth of corporate culture also saw the emergence of company-specific rituals, traditions, and symbols. These elements played a crucial role in reinforcing the values and identity of the organization. For example, IBM had a tradition of the "IBM song," which employees would sing at company events to foster a sense of unity and pride. Similarly, Disney developed a unique corporate culture centered around its mission of creating magical experiences, with employees (known as "cast members") adhering to specific behavioral guidelines and participating in company traditions.

The emphasis on uniformity and conformity in corporate culture had significant implications for employees. On one hand, it provided a clear sense of structure and direction, helping employees understand their roles and responsibilities within the organization. The standardization of work processes and practices also ensured consistency in operations, which could enhance efficiency and productivity.

However, the focus on uniformity and conformity also had its drawbacks. Employees were often expected to suppress their individuality and conform to the norms and values of the organization. This could lead to a sense of alienation and dissatisfaction, as employees felt pressured to conform to a corporate identity that did not align with their personal values and beliefs. The emphasis on conformity could also stifle creativity and innovation, as employees were discouraged from thinking outside the box or challenging the status quo.

The birth of corporate culture also had broader implications for organizations. A strong and cohesive corporate culture could enhance organizational performance by fostering a sense of unity and shared purpose among employees. It could also contribute to a positive reputation and brand image, attracting customers and talent to the organization. However, a rigid and inflexible corporate culture could also hinder adaptability and responsiveness to change, as organizations struggled to break away from established practices and norms.

In the latter half of the 20th century, the concept of corporate culture continued to evolve. The rise of globalization and the information age brought about new challenges and opportunities for organizations. Companies became more diverse and complex, requiring more flexible and adaptive approaches to management. The emphasis on uniformity and conformity began to give way to a greater focus on diversity, inclusivity, and innovation.

The rise of the knowledge economy in the late 20th and early 21st centuries further transformed corporate culture. Knowledge workers, such as software developers, engineers, and consultants, became increasingly important for organizational success. These workers valued autonomy, creativity, and flexibility, leading to a shift in corporate culture towards more open and collaborative work environments. Companies like Google and Apple became known for their innovative and inclusive corporate cultures, which prioritized employee well-being, creativity, and continuous learning.

The digital age has also had a profound impact on corporate culture. Advances in technology, such as the internet, social media, and mobile devices, have transformed the way organizations communicate and operate. The traditional boundaries between work and personal life have become increasingly blurred, leading to new challenges in managing corporate culture. Organizations must now navigate issues related to remote work, digital communication, and the use of social media, while maintaining a cohesive and positive corporate culture.

In recent years, there has been a growing recognition of the importance of corporate social responsibility (CSR) and ethical business practices. Companies are increasingly expected to operate in a socially and environmentally responsible manner, and this has become a key component of corporate culture. Organizations are adopting CSR initiatives, such as sustainability programs, community engagement, and ethical sourcing, to demonstrate their commitment to social and environmental values. This shift reflects a broader trend towards purpose-driven corporate cultures, where organizations prioritize their impact on society and the environment alongside financial performance.

The ongoing evolution of corporate culture also includes a greater focus on diversity, equity, and inclusion (DEI). Organizations are recognizing the importance of creating inclusive work environments that value and respect the diverse backgrounds, perspectives, and experiences of their employees. DEI initiatives aim to address systemic inequalities and create opportunities for underrepresented groups, fostering a more diverse and innovative workforce. This shift towards inclusive corporate cultures is driven by both ethical considerations and the recognition that diversity can enhance organizational performance and innovation.

Chapter 30: Toxic Management

The phenomenon of toxic management, particularly in the form of micromanagement, represents a significant and enduring challenge within modern organizations. Micromanagement, defined as the excessive control and supervision of employees' work and activities, can have profound negative effects on both individuals and organizations. This form of management erodes trust, stifles creativity, reduces job satisfaction, and hampers overall productivity. To fully understand the rise of micromanagement as a form of toxic management, it is essential to explore its historical context, the psychological and organizational factors that contribute to its prevalence, the detrimental impacts on employees and organizations, and the strategies that can be employed to mitigate its effects and promote healthier management practices.

The roots of micromanagement can be traced back to the early management theories of the industrial revolution. During this period, the primary focus was on maximizing efficiency and productivity through standardized processes and strict control of labor. Frederick Winslow Taylor's principles of scientific management, which emerged in the early 20th century, emphasized the importance of detailed task planning, close supervision, and the use of time-and-motion studies to optimize work processes. While these principles were aimed at improving productivity, they also laid the groundwork for a management style characterized by excessive control and oversight.

The rise of large corporations in the 20th century further reinforced the tendency towards micromanagement. As organizations grew in size and complexity, there was an increasing need for formalized structures, policies, and procedures to ensure consistency and control. Hierarchical organizational structures became the norm, with multiple layers of management responsible for overseeing and directing the work of subordinates. In such environments, managers often felt compelled to closely monitor and control the activities of their employees to ensure compliance with established standards and goals.

Psychological factors also play a significant role in the prevalence of micromanagement. One of the key drivers of micromanagement is a lack of trust. Managers who do not trust their employees to perform their tasks effectively may resort to constant supervision and control to ensure that work is completed to their satisfaction. This lack of trust can stem from various sources, including a manager's own insecurities, a history of poor performance among employees, or a corporate culture that emphasizes control and conformity.

Another psychological factor contributing to micromanagement is the desire for control. Managers who have a strong need for control may feel compelled to oversee every aspect of their employees' work to maintain a sense of order and predictability. This need for control can be exacerbated by high levels of stress or pressure to meet organizational goals. In such situations, managers may feel that closely supervising their employees is the only way to ensure that work is completed efficiently and to a high standard.

The rise of micromanagement is also influenced by organizational factors. In highly competitive and fast-paced industries, there is often a significant emphasis on performance and results. This can create a culture of high expectations and constant scrutiny, where managers feel compelled to closely monitor their employees' activities to ensure that targets are met. Additionally, in organizations with rigid hierarchies and bureaucratic structures, there may be a greater tendency towards micromanagement as managers seek to maintain control and authority over their subordinates.

The impact of micromanagement on employees is profoundly negative. One of the most immediate effects is a reduction in job satisfaction. Employees who are subjected to constant supervision and control often feel undervalued and disrespected, leading to a decline in morale and motivation. The lack of autonomy and trust can make employees feel like they are not trusted to perform their jobs effectively, which can lead to frustration and resentment.

Micromanagement also stifles creativity and innovation. When employees are not given the freedom to explore new ideas and approaches, they are less likely to take risks or think outside the box. This can hinder the organization's ability to adapt and innovate in response to changing market conditions or new opportunities. Employees who feel that their ideas and contributions are not valued may also become disengaged and less invested in their work.

Furthermore, micromanagement can lead to increased stress and burnout. The constant pressure to meet the expectations of a micromanaging boss can create a high-stress work environment, where employees feel that they are constantly under scrutiny and must perform perfectly at all times. This can lead to physical and mental health issues, including anxiety, depression, and burnout. The negative impact on employee well-being can, in turn, lead to higher rates of absenteeism and turnover, further affecting organizational performance.

From an organizational perspective, micromanagement can have detrimental effects on overall productivity and performance. While the intention of micromanagement is often to ensure high standards and efficiency, the reality is that it can lead to inefficiencies and reduced productivity. Employees who are constantly monitored may become overly reliant on their managers for direction and decision-making, leading to a lack of initiative and problem-solving skills. This can create a bottleneck effect, where work is delayed because employees are waiting for approval or guidance from their managers.

Micromanagement can also undermine team dynamics and collaboration. In a micromanaged environment, employees may be less likely to collaborate and share ideas, as they may fear criticism or rejection from their manager. This can create a culture of competition and mistrust, where employees are more focused on meeting the expectations of their manager than working together towards common goals. The lack of collaboration and open communication can hinder the organization's ability to leverage the diverse skills and perspectives of its workforce.

To address the issue of micromanagement and promote healthier management practices, organizations need to adopt a multifaceted approach. One of the key strategies is to build a culture of trust and empowerment. This involves creating an environment where employees feel trusted and valued, and where they are given the autonomy and support to perform their jobs effectively. Managers should focus on providing clear expectations and goals, while allowing employees the freedom to determine the best way to achieve them. This can help to foster a sense of ownership and accountability, and encourage employees to take initiative and develop their problem-solving skills.

Effective communication is also essential in addressing micromanagement. Managers should strive to maintain open and transparent communication with their employees, providing regular feedback and support while also listening to their concerns and ideas. This can help to build trust and mutual respect, and ensure that employees feel heard and valued. Additionally, managers should provide constructive feedback and coaching, rather than constantly monitoring and correcting employees' work. This can help to build employees' confidence and competence, and reduce the need for micromanagement.

Training and development programs can also play a crucial role in addressing micromanagement. Organizations should provide training for managers on effective leadership and management practices, including how to delegate effectively, build trust, and foster a positive work environment. This can help managers to develop the skills and confidence needed to manage their teams without resorting to micromanagement. Additionally, organizations should provide opportunities for employees to develop their skills and capabilities, so that they feel confident and competent in their roles.

Another important strategy is to create a supportive and inclusive work environment. This involves fostering a culture of collaboration and teamwork, where employees feel comfortable sharing ideas and working together towards common goals. Organizations should also promote work-life balance and employee well-being, recognizing that a healthy and engaged workforce is essential for organizational success. This can include providing flexible work arrangements, promoting wellness programs, and encouraging employees to take breaks and time off to recharge.

Chapter 31: Digital Leashes

The concept of "digital leashes" refers to the phenomenon where employees are perpetually connected to their work through digital devices and platforms, making them always reachable and, in effect, always working. This perpetual connectivity, driven by advances in technology, has transformed the nature of work and the boundaries between professional and personal life. The implications of digital leashes are profound, impacting employee well-being, work-life balance, productivity, and organizational culture. To thoroughly understand the rise of the always-connected employee, it is essential to explore the historical context, the factors that have contributed to this trend, its effects on workers and organizations, and potential strategies to mitigate its negative consequences.

The rise of digital leashes can be traced back to the advent of the internet and the proliferation of digital communication technologies in the late 20th and early 21st centuries. The introduction of email, mobile phones, and later, smartphones, revolutionized the way people communicate and work. These technologies enabled instant communication and access to information, significantly increasing the efficiency and speed of business operations. However, they also began to blur the boundaries between work and personal life, as employees could now be reached anytime and anywhere.

The widespread adoption of smartphones in the early 2000s marked a significant turning point in the emergence of digital leashes. Smartphones combined the functionalities of mobile phones, email, and internet access, allowing employees to stay connected to their work even when they were away from their desks. This constant connectivity was further amplified by the development of various communication and collaboration tools, such as instant messaging, video conferencing, and project management platforms. These tools facilitated real-time communication and collaboration, making it possible for employees to work remotely and stay connected with their teams at all times.

The rise of remote work and the gig economy has further entrenched the concept of digital leashes. Advances in technology have made it possible for employees to work from anywhere, leading to an increase in remote and flexible work arrangements. While these arrangements offer numerous benefits, such as greater flexibility and autonomy, they also contribute to the expectation that employees are always available and reachable. In the gig economy, where workers often juggle multiple jobs and clients, the pressure to stay connected and responsive can be even more pronounced.

One of the key factors contributing to the prevalence of digital leashes is the growing emphasis on productivity and responsiveness in the modern workplace. In a highly competitive and fast-paced business environment, organizations place a premium on speed and efficiency. Employees are often expected to respond to emails, messages, and calls promptly, regardless of the time or their location. This expectation is reinforced by organizational cultures that value responsiveness and availability, often rewarding those who are always connected and quick to respond.

The COVID-19 pandemic has also played a significant role in accelerating the trend of always-connected employees. The sudden shift to remote work during the pandemic forced organizations to adopt digital communication and collaboration tools on an unprecedented scale. While these tools enabled business continuity, they also intensified the blurring of boundaries between work and personal life. With many employees working from home, the physical separation between work and personal spaces diminished, leading to longer working hours and an increased expectation of constant availability.

The implications of digital leashes for employees are profound and multifaceted. One of the most significant effects is on work-life balance. The constant connectivity and expectation of availability can make it difficult for employees to disconnect from work and fully engage in personal and family activities. This blurring of boundaries can lead to an "always-on" culture, where employees feel pressured to be available and responsive at all times, even during evenings, weekends, and vacations. The inability to disconnect from work can result in increased stress and burnout, negatively impacting employees' mental and physical health.

The perpetual connectivity associated with digital leashes can also erode the quality of personal relationships. When employees are constantly checking their emails, messages, or work-related notifications, it can create a sense of intrusion into their personal lives. This can lead to feelings of frustration and resentment among family members and friends, as employees are often distracted or preoccupied with work even during personal time. The inability to fully disconnect from work can also lead to a lack of meaningful relaxation and leisure time, further exacerbating stress and burnout.

From a productivity perspective, the impact of digital leashes is complex. On one hand, constant connectivity can enhance efficiency and responsiveness, enabling employees to address work-related issues promptly and collaborate effectively with their teams. This can lead to improved performance and productivity, especially in fast-paced and dynamic work environments. On the other hand, the constant interruptions and distractions caused by digital leashes can hinder deep work and focus. Employees may find it challenging to concentrate on complex tasks or engage in creative thinking when they are frequently interrupted by emails, messages, or notifications. This can lead to a decline in overall productivity and job satisfaction.

The impact of digital leashes on organizational culture is also significant. Organizations that foster an always-on culture may inadvertently create an environment of high stress and burnout. Employees may feel that they are expected to be constantly available and responsive, leading to a culture of overwork and presenteeism. This can result in high turnover rates, as employees seek healthier work environments that respect their boundaries and prioritize work-life balance. Additionally, organizations that do not address the negative impacts of digital leashes may struggle to attract and retain top talent, as prospective employees increasingly value flexibility and well-being.

To mitigate the negative consequences of digital leashes and promote a healthier work environment, organizations can adopt several strategies. One of the key approaches is to establish clear boundaries and expectations around work hours and availability. Organizations should communicate the importance of work-life balance and encourage employees to disconnect from work during non-working hours. This can be achieved through policies that limit after-hours emails and messages, as well as promoting the use of out-of-office notifications and autoresponders.

Another important strategy is to foster a culture of trust and autonomy. Organizations should empower employees to manage their own time and work schedules, allowing them to determine when and how they are most productive. This can help reduce the pressure to be constantly connected and responsive, as employees are given the flexibility to work in a way that suits their individual needs and preferences. Managers should focus on outcomes and results, rather than monitoring employees' availability or responsiveness.

Providing employees with the tools and resources to manage their digital workload effectively is also crucial. This includes training on time management, digital well-being, and the use of productivity tools that can help reduce the burden of constant connectivity. Organizations can also implement technology solutions that help manage digital distractions, such as tools that limit notifications or enable focused work sessions. Encouraging employees to take regular breaks and disconnect from work can also help promote well-being and prevent burnout.

Leadership plays a critical role in addressing the issue of digital leashes. Leaders should model healthy work behaviors and set an example by respecting boundaries and promoting work-life balance. This includes avoiding sending emails or messages outside of work hours and encouraging employees to take time off and disconnect from work. Leaders should also be proactive in addressing issues related to digital overload and stress, providing support and resources to help employees manage their workload and well-being.

Chapter 32: Burnout Epidemic

The burnout epidemic is a significant and pervasive issue in the modern workplace, affecting employees across various industries and job roles. Burnout, defined as a state of physical, emotional, and mental exhaustion caused by prolonged and excessive stress, has become increasingly common in today's fast-paced and demanding work environments. The implications of burnout are far-reaching, impacting not only individual well-being but also organizational performance, productivity, and overall workplace culture. To comprehensively understand the burnout epidemic, it is essential to explore its historical context, the factors contributing to its rise, its effects on employees and organizations, and the strategies that can be employed to address and prevent burnout in the workplace.

The concept of burnout was first introduced by psychologist Herbert Freudenberger in the 1970s. Freudenberger observed that individuals in high-stress professions, such as healthcare and social work, were experiencing chronic exhaustion, cynicism, and a sense of inefficacy. He coined the term "burnout" to describe this phenomenon and highlighted the need for further research and understanding of its causes and effects. Since then, burnout has been widely studied and recognized as a significant occupational hazard, affecting workers in various fields.

Several factors contribute to the rise of burnout in the modern workplace. One of the primary factors is the increasing demands and pressures placed on employees. In today's competitive and fast-paced business environment, employees are often expected to perform at high levels, meet tight deadlines, and achieve ambitious targets. This pressure to constantly deliver results can lead to prolonged periods of stress and exhaustion, making employees more susceptible to burnout.

The advent of digital technology and the rise of the always-connected workplace have also played a significant role in the burnout epidemic. With the proliferation of smartphones, emails, and instant messaging, employees are often expected to be available and responsive at all times, even outside of traditional working hours. This constant connectivity blurs the boundaries between work and personal life, making it difficult for employees to disconnect and recharge. The pressure to stay connected and responsive can lead to chronic stress and burnout over time.

Another contributing factor to burnout is the lack of control and autonomy that many employees experience in their jobs. When employees feel that they have little control over their work tasks, schedules, or decision-making processes, they are more likely to experience stress and frustration. This lack of autonomy can lead to feelings of helplessness and inefficacy, which are key components of burnout. Additionally, employees who feel that their efforts are not recognized or valued by their organization are more likely to experience burnout, as they may perceive their work as meaningless or unrewarding.

Workplace culture and organizational practices also play a crucial role in the prevalence of burnout. In some organizations, there is a culture of overwork and presenteeism, where employees feel that they are expected to work long hours and be constantly available to demonstrate their commitment and dedication. This culture can create an environment of high stress and burnout, as employees feel pressured to prioritize work over their personal well-being. Furthermore, organizations that do not provide adequate support and resources for employee well-being, such as mental health services, flexible work arrangements, and opportunities for rest and recovery, are more likely to experience high levels of burnout among their workforce.

The effects of burnout on employees are profound and multifaceted. One of the most immediate and noticeable effects is physical exhaustion. Employees experiencing burnout often report feeling constantly tired and lacking energy, even after resting. This physical exhaustion can lead to a decline in overall health, as individuals may neglect their physical well-being, engage in unhealthy behaviors, and experience a weakened immune system. Chronic exhaustion can also result in sleep disturbances, which further exacerbate the cycle of stress and burnout.

Burnout also has significant emotional and psychological effects on employees. Individuals experiencing burnout often report feelings of cynicism, detachment, and a lack of motivation. They may become disengaged from their work, feeling that their efforts are futile or unappreciated. This emotional exhaustion can lead to a decline in job satisfaction and overall well-being, as employees struggle to find meaning and fulfillment in their work. Additionally, burnout is closely linked to mental health issues such as anxiety, depression, and stress-related disorders. Employees experiencing burnout are more likely to report symptoms of these conditions, which can further impact their ability to function effectively in both their personal and professional lives.

The cognitive effects of burnout are also significant. Burnout can impair an individual's ability to concentrate, make decisions, and solve problems. This cognitive decline can lead to decreased productivity and performance, as employees struggle to complete tasks efficiently and effectively. Furthermore, burnout can impact an individual's creativity and innovation, as chronic stress and exhaustion stifle the ability to think critically and generate new ideas.

From an organizational perspective, the burnout epidemic has far-reaching implications. High levels of burnout among employees can lead to decreased productivity and performance, as individuals struggle to meet their job responsibilities. This decline in performance can result in increased errors, reduced quality of work, and missed deadlines, all of which can negatively impact the organization's overall success and competitiveness. Additionally, burnout can lead to higher rates of absenteeism and turnover, as employees take time off to recover or leave the organization in search of healthier work environments. The costs associated with burnout, including lost productivity, recruitment, and training, can be significant for organizations.

The burnout epidemic also has broader implications for workplace culture and employee engagement. In organizations where burnout is prevalent, there is often a culture of high stress and low morale. Employees may feel that their well-being is not a priority for the organization, leading to disengagement and a lack of loyalty. This disengagement can create a negative feedback loop, where decreased motivation and performance further contribute to the cycle of burnout. Additionally, a culture of burnout can hinder collaboration and teamwork, as employees become more focused on their individual stressors and less likely to support and engage with their colleagues.

To address and prevent burnout in the workplace, organizations must adopt a comprehensive and multifaceted approach. One of the key strategies is to promote work-life balance and encourage employees to take breaks and time off to rest and recharge. This can include implementing policies that limit after-hours emails and messages, promoting the use of vacation time, and offering flexible work arrangements. Organizations should also provide resources and support for employee well-being, such as mental health services, wellness programs, and opportunities for physical activity and relaxation.

Another important strategy is to foster a culture of recognition and appreciation. Employees who feel that their efforts are valued and recognized are more likely to experience job satisfaction and motivation. Organizations can promote a culture of appreciation by regularly acknowledging and rewarding employees' contributions, providing opportunities for growth and development, and creating a supportive and inclusive work environment.

Additionally, organizations should prioritize employee autonomy and control. Providing employees with the flexibility to manage their own schedules, make decisions about their work tasks, and contribute to organizational goals can help reduce feelings of helplessness and inefficacy. This can be achieved through practices such as participative decision-making, empowering employees to take ownership of their work, and providing opportunities for skill development and career advancement.

Leadership also plays a crucial role in addressing and preventing burnout. Leaders should model healthy work behaviors and set an example by prioritizing their own well-being and encouraging their teams to do the same. This includes promoting work-life balance, recognizing and addressing signs of burnout, and providing support and resources for employees' well-being. Effective leadership also involves creating an open and transparent communication culture, where employees feel comfortable discussing their stressors and challenges without fear of judgment or reprisal.

Training and education are also essential components of addressing burnout. Organizations should provide training for employees and managers on recognizing the signs of burnout, managing stress, and promoting mental health and well-being. This can include workshops, seminars, and online resources that provide practical strategies and tools for managing stress and preventing burnout. Additionally, organizations should promote awareness and destigmatize mental health issues, encouraging employees to seek help and support when needed.

Chapter 33: Gender Disparities: Women in the Workforce

Gender disparities in the workforce remain a persistent and complex issue, reflecting broader societal inequalities and cultural norms that have evolved over centuries. Despite significant progress towards gender equality, women continue to face numerous challenges and barriers that affect their participation, advancement, and treatment in the workplace. These disparities manifest in various forms, including wage gaps, underrepresentation in leadership positions, occupational segregation, and workplace discrimination. Understanding the historical context, contributing factors, and impacts of gender disparities, as well as exploring strategies to address and overcome these challenges, is crucial for fostering a more equitable and inclusive workforce.

Historically, the role of women in the workforce has been shaped by cultural, social, and economic factors. For much of history, societal norms and legal restrictions limited women's participation in paid work, confining them primarily to domestic roles. The industrial revolution in the 18th and 19th centuries marked a significant shift, as economic changes necessitated women's entry into the labor force, particularly in factories and service industries. However, women were often relegated to low-paying, low-status jobs, and their work was undervalued compared to that of men.

The early 20th century saw the rise of the women's suffrage movement, which advocated for women's right to vote and broader gender equality. This movement laid the groundwork for subsequent advances in women's rights and workplace participation. During World War II, women entered the workforce in unprecedented numbers to fill roles left vacant by men who had gone to fight. This period demonstrated women's capabilities in various occupations, challenging traditional gender roles. However, after the war, many women were pushed back into domestic roles or lower-paying jobs as men returned to the workforce.

The latter half of the 20th century brought significant legislative and social changes aimed at promoting gender equality. The civil rights movement, the feminist movement, and various anti-discrimination laws, such as the Equal Pay Act of 1963 and the Civil Rights Act of 1964 in the United States, sought to address gender disparities in the workplace. These efforts led to increased opportunities for women in education and employment, and a gradual narrowing of the gender wage gap. Despite these advancements, substantial disparities persisted, necessitating ongoing efforts to achieve true gender equality.

One of the most prominent manifestations of gender disparities in the workforce is the gender wage gap. On average, women earn less than men for the same work, a discrepancy that persists across industries, occupations, and regions. Various factors contribute to the gender wage gap, including occupational segregation, differences in work experience and education, and discrimination. Women are often concentrated in lower-paying occupations and industries, such as education, healthcare, and service roles, while men dominate higher-paying fields like technology, engineering, and finance. Even within the same occupations, women frequently earn less than their male counterparts due to differences in negotiation outcomes, career interruptions for caregiving responsibilities, and bias in promotion and compensation practices.

Another significant issue is the underrepresentation of women in leadership positions. Despite comprising nearly half of the workforce in many countries, women are significantly underrepresented in senior management and executive roles. This disparity is often referred to as the "glass ceiling," a metaphor for the invisible barriers that prevent women from advancing to the highest levels of organizational leadership. Factors contributing to the glass ceiling include gender bias, lack of mentorship and sponsorship, and organizational cultures that favor traditionally masculine leadership traits. Women often face greater scrutiny and higher standards for performance, and their leadership styles may be undervalued or misunderstood.

Occupational segregation also plays a critical role in perpetuating gender disparities. Horizontal segregation refers to the concentration of men and women in different occupations, while vertical segregation involves the stratification of genders within the same occupation, with men typically occupying higher-status and better-paying roles. This segregation is influenced by societal norms and stereotypes about gender roles, which shape educational and career choices from an early age. For example, girls may be discouraged from pursuing studies in science, technology, engineering, and mathematics (STEM) fields, leading to lower representation of women in these high-paying and high-growth industries.

Workplace discrimination and harassment further exacerbate gender disparities. Women often face bias in hiring, promotion, and performance evaluations, as well as discriminatory practices such as unequal pay for equal work. Sexual harassment remains a pervasive issue, creating hostile work environments that undermine women's safety, well-being, and career progression. The #MeToo movement has brought significant attention to these issues, highlighting the need for systemic changes to address and prevent harassment and discrimination in the workplace.

The impact of gender disparities extends beyond individual employees to affect organizational performance and economic growth. Research has shown that diverse and inclusive workplaces, where women are represented at all levels, tend to perform better financially and are more innovative. Organizations that leverage the full potential of their talent pool, regardless of gender, benefit from diverse perspectives and ideas, which can drive creativity and problem-solving. Moreover, closing the gender gap in labor force participation and earnings can lead to substantial economic gains. According to estimates by the McKinsey Global Institute, advancing gender equality could add trillions of dollars to global GDP by 2025.

Addressing gender disparities in the workforce requires a multifaceted approach that involves policy changes, organizational practices, and cultural shifts. One of the key strategies is to promote equal pay for equal work. Governments and organizations can implement pay transparency measures, conduct regular pay audits, and enforce anti-discrimination laws to ensure that women are compensated fairly. Additionally, supporting women's career advancement through mentorship, sponsorship, and leadership development programs can help break the glass ceiling and increase women's representation in senior roles.

Creating family-friendly workplace policies is also essential for promoting gender equality. Offering flexible work arrangements, paid parental leave, and affordable childcare options can help women balance work and caregiving responsibilities, reducing career interruptions and enabling greater participation in the workforce. These policies benefit not only women but also men, promoting a more equitable distribution of caregiving responsibilities and challenging traditional gender roles.

Educational initiatives play a crucial role in addressing occupational segregation and encouraging more women to pursue careers in high-paying and high-growth fields. Programs that promote STEM education for girls, provide career guidance, and offer scholarships and mentorship opportunities can help bridge the gender gap in these industries. Organizations can also create inclusive hiring and promotion practices that value diverse skills and experiences, rather than relying on traditional criteria that may favor men.

Fostering inclusive organizational cultures is fundamental to addressing gender disparities. This involves creating environments where diverse perspectives are valued, bias and discrimination are actively challenged, and all employees feel safe and respected. Implementing diversity and inclusion training, establishing clear anti-harassment policies, and encouraging open dialogue about gender issues can help build a more inclusive workplace. Leadership commitment is critical, as leaders set the tone for organizational culture and can drive meaningful change through their actions and policies.

The role of men in promoting gender equality should not be overlooked. Engaging men as allies in the effort to achieve gender parity is essential for creating lasting change. Men can advocate for equal opportunities, challenge discriminatory practices, and support policies that promote work-life balance and caregiving responsibilities. By working together, men and women can create more equitable and inclusive workplaces that benefit everyone.

Chapter 34: The Work-Life Balance Myth

The concept of work-life balance has become a prominent topic of discussion in the modern workplace, touted as a key to achieving personal well-being and professional success. However, for many employees, the pursuit of a perfect work-life balance often feels like chasing an elusive ideal, leading to frustration and disillusionment. The notion of work-life balance suggests a harmonious equilibrium between work responsibilities and personal life, but the reality for most people is far more complex. The challenges of achieving this balance are influenced by various factors, including societal expectations, organizational cultures, economic pressures, and technological advancements. Understanding the intricacies of the work-life balance myth, the struggles faced by modern employees, and potential strategies to navigate these challenges is essential for fostering a more realistic and sustainable approach to integrating work and life.

The idea of work-life balance emerged in the latter half of the 20th century as a response to the increasing demands of work and the evolving roles of men and women in society. The traditional model of work, characterized by rigid schedules and clear boundaries between work and personal life, began to shift with the rise of dual-income households and the growing participation of women in the workforce. This shift necessitated a reevaluation of how individuals manage their time and responsibilities, leading to the popularization of work-life balance as a desirable goal.

Despite its widespread appeal, the concept of work-life balance is inherently flawed in several ways. Firstly, it implies a static equilibrium where work and life are evenly distributed, which is rarely achievable in practice. Life is dynamic, and the demands of work and personal life can fluctuate greatly, making a perfectly balanced state unrealistic.

Secondly, the notion of balance suggests a clear separation between work and life, which is increasingly difficult to maintain in an era where technology blurs these boundaries. Lastly, the emphasis on balance can create pressure and guilt for individuals who struggle to achieve it, leading to feelings of inadequacy and stress.

One of the primary challenges in achieving work-life balance is the increasing demands and expectations placed on employees. In today's competitive and fast-paced business environment, organizations often expect high levels of performance, productivity, and availability. Employees may feel pressured to work long hours, meet tight deadlines, and continuously improve their skills and performance. This pressure is exacerbated by economic factors such as job insecurity, financial instability, and the need to maintain a certain standard of living. As a result, many employees find it difficult to carve out time for personal and family life, leading to an imbalance that favors work.

Technological advancements have further complicated the pursuit of work-life balance. The proliferation of smartphones, laptops, and other digital devices has made it possible for employees to stay connected to work at all times. While these technologies offer flexibility and convenience, they also create an expectation of constant availability. Emails, messages, and notifications can intrude into personal time, making it challenging for employees to disconnect from work. The blurring of boundaries between work and personal life can lead to longer working hours, increased stress, and reduced quality of life.

Societal and cultural expectations also play a significant role in shaping the struggles of modern employees. Traditional gender roles and societal norms often place disproportionate caregiving and household responsibilities on women, even as they pursue careers. This "second shift" phenomenon means that many women are effectively working two jobs—one in the workplace and one at home. Men, too, face pressures to conform to societal expectations of being the primary breadwinner, which can lead to long working hours and limited time for family and personal pursuits. These gendered expectations can make it difficult for both men and women to achieve a balanced integration of work and life.

Organizational cultures and practices can either support or hinder employees' efforts to achieve work-life balance. In some organizations, there is a culture of overwork and presenteeism, where employees feel that they are expected to be always on and available. This culture can create an environment of high stress and burnout, as employees struggle to meet these expectations while managing their personal lives. Additionally, organizations that do not provide adequate support for work-life balance, such as flexible work arrangements, parental leave, and wellness programs, can exacerbate the challenges faced by employees.

The impact of work-life imbalance on employees is profound and multifaceted. One of the most immediate and noticeable effects is physical and mental exhaustion. Long working hours and the inability to disconnect from work can lead to chronic stress, fatigue, and burnout. Employees may experience a decline in their overall health, with increased risks of conditions such as anxiety, depression, cardiovascular diseases, and sleep disorders. The stress of managing work and personal responsibilities can also lead to emotional and psychological strain, affecting relationships with family and friends.

Work-life imbalance can also have significant implications for employee productivity and performance. When employees are overworked and stressed, their ability to concentrate, make decisions, and solve problems can be impaired. This cognitive decline can lead to decreased productivity, increased errors, and reduced quality of work. Furthermore, employees who are unable to balance work and personal life may experience a decline in job satisfaction and motivation, leading to disengagement and a lack of commitment to their work and organization.

The consequences of work-life imbalance extend beyond individual employees to affect organizational performance and success. High levels of stress and burnout among employees can lead to increased absenteeism, turnover, and healthcare costs. Organizations may struggle to attract and retain top talent if they are perceived as not supporting work-life balance. Additionally, a culture of overwork and stress can hinder collaboration, innovation, and overall organizational morale, ultimately impacting the organization's bottom line.

To address the challenges of work-life balance and support the well-being of employees, organizations can adopt several strategies. One of the key approaches is to promote flexible work arrangements. This can include options such as remote work, flexible hours, compressed workweeks, and job sharing. Flexible work arrangements allow employees to manage their work schedules in a way that accommodates their personal and family responsibilities, reducing the stress of balancing competing demands.

Providing adequate support for employees' personal and family needs is also crucial. This can include offering generous parental leave policies, providing access to affordable childcare, and creating family-friendly workplace practices. Organizations can also support employees' mental and physical well-being through wellness programs, mental health resources, and opportunities for relaxation and recreation. Encouraging employees to take regular breaks, vacations, and time off to recharge can help prevent burnout and promote a healthier work-life integration.

Creating a supportive organizational culture is fundamental to addressing work-life balance challenges. Leaders and managers play a critical role in setting the tone for the organization's culture and practices. By modeling healthy work behaviors, such as setting boundaries, taking breaks, and prioritizing well-being, leaders can encourage employees to do the same. Open communication about work-life balance, recognition of employees' efforts, and support for personal and family needs can foster a culture of trust and respect.

It is also important to recognize that work-life balance is not a one-size-fits-all concept. Different employees have different needs and priorities, and what works for one person may not work for another. Organizations should adopt a personalized approach to work-life balance, allowing employees to tailor their work arrangements and support to their individual circumstances. This can involve regular check-ins with employees, gathering feedback on their needs and preferences, and providing a range of options and resources to support their well-being.

Addressing societal and cultural norms is also essential for promoting work-life balance. This involves challenging traditional gender roles and expectations, promoting gender equality, and encouraging shared responsibilities for caregiving and household tasks. By creating an environment where both men and women can pursue careers and personal life without undue pressure or bias, organizations can support a more balanced and inclusive workforce.

Chapter 35: Remote Work: Freedom or New Chains?

Remote work has emerged as a significant trend in the modern workplace, accelerated by advancements in technology and the global COVID-19 pandemic. This mode of work offers the promise of greater freedom and flexibility, allowing employees to work from anywhere, avoid lengthy commutes, and tailor their schedules to better fit their personal lives. However, the reality of remote work is complex, and for many, it comes with its own set of challenges and constraints. While remote work can indeed provide a sense of liberation from traditional office environments, it can also introduce new forms of pressure, isolation, and blurred boundaries between work and personal life. Understanding the dual nature of remote work—its potential for freedom and its propensity to create new chains—is essential for navigating this evolving landscape.

The rise of remote work can be traced back to the proliferation of digital technologies and the internet in the late 20th and early 21st centuries. With the advent of email, video conferencing, cloud computing, and collaborative software, the necessity of physical presence in the workplace began to diminish. Companies started to recognize the benefits of remote work, such as cost savings on office space and the ability to attract talent from a broader geographic area. The COVID-19 pandemic in 2020 further accelerated this trend, as lockdowns and social distancing measures forced many organizations to adopt remote work on an unprecedented scale. This shift demonstrated that many jobs could be effectively performed outside of traditional office settings, leading to a reevaluation of work practices and norms.

One of the most significant advantages of remote work is the flexibility it offers. Employees can often set their own schedules, allowing them to work at times when they are most productive or when it best fits their personal lives. This flexibility can lead to improved work-life balance, as individuals can more easily manage their professional responsibilities alongside personal and family commitments. The elimination of daily commutes also saves time and reduces stress, contributing to overall well-being. Additionally, remote work can provide opportunities for individuals who may face challenges in a traditional office environment, such as those with disabilities, caregivers, or people living in remote areas.

Remote work also opens up new possibilities for organizations. Companies can reduce overhead costs associated with maintaining physical office spaces and can access a larger talent pool by hiring employees from different regions or even different countries. This geographic diversity can bring new perspectives and ideas, fostering innovation and creativity. Furthermore, remote work can enhance employee satisfaction and retention, as workers appreciate the autonomy and flexibility it provides. Organizations that embrace remote work can position themselves as forward-thinking and adaptable, attracting top talent and staying competitive in a rapidly changing business landscape.

Despite these benefits, remote work also introduces several challenges that can undermine its potential advantages. One of the primary issues is the blurring of boundaries between work and personal life. When work takes place in the same environment as daily living, it can be difficult to separate the two, leading to longer working hours and difficulty disconnecting from work. This blurring of boundaries can contribute to stress, burnout, and a sense of being constantly "on," as employees struggle to establish clear demarcations between their professional and personal time.

Isolation and loneliness are significant concerns for remote workers. The absence of face-to-face interactions with colleagues can lead to feelings of disconnection and social isolation. While digital communication tools can facilitate collaboration and communication, they often lack the richness and spontaneity of in-person interactions. The informal conversations and social bonding that occur in a traditional office setting can be harder to replicate in a remote environment, potentially impacting team cohesion and morale. For some employees, the lack of social interaction can affect mental health and well-being, leading to feelings of loneliness and disengagement.

Remote work can also exacerbate issues related to communication and collaboration. In a remote setting, effective communication relies heavily on digital tools, which can sometimes lead to misunderstandings or misinterpretations. The lack of nonverbal cues, such as body language and facial expressions, can make it harder to convey tone and intent. Additionally, coordinating work across different time zones and schedules can be challenging, requiring careful planning and flexibility. Without the natural opportunities for collaboration that occur in an office environment, remote teams may struggle to maintain alignment and cohesion, potentially impacting productivity and innovation.

Performance management and career development are other areas that can be impacted by remote work. Managers may find it challenging to monitor and assess employee performance in a remote setting, relying on output rather than process. This shift can be beneficial, promoting a focus on results rather than hours worked, but it can also lead to concerns about fairness and visibility. Remote workers may worry about being overlooked for promotions and opportunities due to their physical absence from the office. Ensuring that remote employees receive adequate feedback, support, and development opportunities requires intentional effort and strategies from managers and organizations.

The home environment itself can present challenges for remote work. Not all employees have access to a dedicated, quiet workspace, which can impact productivity and focus. Distractions from family members, household chores, and other domestic responsibilities can make it difficult to maintain a consistent work routine. Additionally, the costs associated with setting up a home office, such as purchasing equipment and ensuring reliable internet connectivity, can be a burden for some employees. Organizations that do not provide adequate support for these needs may inadvertently create disparities among their remote workforce.

To address these challenges and harness the benefits of remote work, organizations and employees must adopt strategies that promote a healthy and sustainable remote work environment. One key approach is to establish clear boundaries between work and personal life. This can involve setting specific work hours, creating a dedicated workspace, and implementing rituals or routines that signal the start and end of the workday. Encouraging employees to take regular breaks and time off is also important for preventing burnout and maintaining well-being.

Effective communication and collaboration are critical in a remote work setting. Organizations can invest in robust digital tools and platforms that facilitate seamless communication and collaboration. Regular check-ins, team meetings, and virtual social activities can help maintain connection and cohesion among remote workers. Providing training and resources on best practices for remote communication can also help employees navigate the challenges of digital interactions.

Support for mental health and well-being is essential for remote workers. Organizations can offer resources such as counseling services, wellness programs, and access to mental health professionals. Creating a culture that prioritizes well-being and encourages employees to seek help when needed can help mitigate the impacts of isolation and stress. Managers can play a key role by regularly checking in with their team members, offering support, and promoting a healthy work-life balance.

Performance management and career development in a remote work environment require intentional effort and strategies. Organizations can implement clear and transparent performance metrics that focus on outcomes rather than hours worked. Regular feedback and development discussions can help remote employees feel valued and supported. Providing opportunities for skill development, training, and mentorship can also ensure that remote workers have access to career advancement and growth.

Equity and inclusion are important considerations in a remote work setting. Organizations must ensure that remote employees have access to the resources and support they need to succeed. This can include providing equipment and technology, offering stipends for home office setup, and ensuring that all employees have access to the same opportunities and benefits. Creating an inclusive culture that values and supports remote work can help mitigate disparities and ensure that all employees feel valued and included.

Chapter 36: Automation and AI: The Future of Employment

The advent of automation and artificial intelligence (AI) represents a paradigm shift in the future of employment, poised to transform industries and redefine the nature of work. Automation refers to the use of machines and technology to perform tasks that were once done manually, while AI encompasses the creation of intelligent systems that can learn, reason, and make decisions. Together, these technologies promise unprecedented efficiencies and capabilities, but they also pose significant challenges and uncertainties. As society stands on the brink of this technological revolution, it is essential to explore the potential impacts of automation and AI on employment, considering both the opportunities they present and the complex issues they raise.

The history of automation dates back to the Industrial Revolution, when mechanization began to replace manual labor in various sectors. However, the scale and sophistication of modern automation and AI far surpass anything seen in the past. Advances in robotics, machine learning, and data analytics have enabled machines to perform a wide array of tasks, from manufacturing and logistics to customer service and decision-making. The rapid pace of technological development means that jobs once considered safe from automation are now vulnerable, leading to concerns about widespread job displacement and economic disruption.

One of the primary opportunities presented by automation and AI is increased productivity. Automated systems can operate continuously without breaks, fatigue, or errors, leading to higher output and efficiency. In manufacturing, for example, robots can assemble products with precision and speed, reducing production costs and improving quality. In the service sector, AI-powered chatbots and virtual assistants can handle customer inquiries around the clock, providing instant responses and freeing human workers for more complex tasks. The increased productivity driven by automation and AI has the potential to boost economic growth and competitiveness.

Automation and AI also have the potential to enhance workplace safety. In industries such as mining, construction, and manufacturing, automation can take over hazardous tasks, reducing the risk of accidents and injuries. Autonomous vehicles, for instance, can navigate dangerous environments, transport materials, and perform inspections without putting human workers at risk. AI can also be used to monitor workplace conditions, predict potential safety hazards, and implement preventive measures. By reducing the need for humans to engage in dangerous work, automation and AI can contribute to a safer and healthier work environment.

Another significant opportunity lies in the potential for job creation in new fields. The development and deployment of automation and AI technologies require a range of skills and expertise, leading to the creation of new jobs in areas such as robotics engineering, data science, AI research, and cybersecurity. Additionally, as automation and AI take over routine and repetitive tasks, human workers can focus on more creative, strategic, and value-added activities. This shift could lead to the emergence of new roles and industries that capitalize on uniquely human capabilities, such as empathy, critical thinking, and innovation.

Despite these opportunities, the rise of automation and AI also raises significant concerns about job displacement and inequality. As machines and algorithms become capable of performing tasks traditionally done by humans, many jobs are at risk of becoming obsolete. Routine and repetitive jobs, such as assembly line work, data entry, and telemarketing, are particularly vulnerable to automation. However, advancements in AI mean that even more complex tasks, such as financial analysis, legal research, and medical diagnostics, are increasingly being performed by intelligent systems. The potential for widespread job displacement poses a major challenge for workers, industries, and policymakers.

The impact of automation and AI on employment is not uniform across all sectors and regions. Certain industries, such as manufacturing and transportation, are more susceptible to automation, while others, such as healthcare and education, may be less affected in the short term. The regional impact also varies, with areas that are heavily reliant on manufacturing or routine jobs likely to experience more significant disruption. Additionally, workers with lower levels of education and skills are more vulnerable to job displacement, exacerbating existing inequalities and creating new divides in the labor market.

The potential for job displacement due to automation and AI raises critical questions about the future of work and the role of human labor. One of the key challenges is how to manage the transition for displaced workers. Reskilling and upskilling programs are essential to equip workers with the skills needed for new roles in the evolving job market. This requires investment in education and training, as well as partnerships between governments, businesses, and educational institutions. Lifelong learning and continuous professional development will become increasingly important as the pace of technological change accelerates.

Social safety nets and labor policies also need to adapt to the changing landscape of work. Unemployment benefits, income support, and retraining programs are crucial to help displaced workers navigate periods of transition and uncertainty. Policymakers must consider how to design social protection systems that are responsive to the challenges posed by automation and AI, ensuring that workers are not left behind. Additionally, labor laws and regulations may need to be updated to address issues such as job security, worker rights, and fair wages in an increasingly automated economy.

The rise of automation and AI also raises ethical and societal questions about the nature of work and the distribution of wealth. As machines and algorithms take over more tasks, the definition of work may need to be reexamined. The traditional model of full-time, stable employment may become less common, with more workers engaging in freelance, gig, or project-based work. This shift has implications for job security, benefits, and worker protections. Additionally, the economic gains from increased productivity and efficiency must be distributed fairly to prevent widening inequality. Policymakers and business leaders must consider how to ensure that the benefits of automation and AI are shared broadly across society.

The integration of AI into the workplace also raises concerns about privacy and surveillance. AI systems often rely on large amounts of data to function effectively, leading to the collection and analysis of personal and professional information. This data can be used to monitor employee performance, track productivity, and even predict behaviors. While these capabilities can enhance efficiency and decision-making, they also raise ethical questions about worker privacy and autonomy. Organizations must navigate the balance between leveraging AI for performance management and respecting employees' rights to privacy and dignity.

The future of employment in an era of automation and AI is likely to involve a hybrid model where humans and machines work together. Collaborative robots, or cobots, are designed to work alongside human workers, augmenting their capabilities and taking over repetitive or dangerous tasks. In professional settings, AI can assist with data analysis, decision-making, and customer service, allowing human workers to focus on strategic and creative activities. This symbiotic relationship between humans and machines has the potential to enhance productivity and innovation, but it requires careful management to ensure that workers are supported and valued.

Education and training systems must evolve to prepare the workforce for the demands of an automated and AI-driven economy. Emphasizing STEM (science, technology, engineering, and mathematics) education is important, but so is fostering skills in areas such as critical thinking, creativity, and emotional intelligence. These human-centric skills are less likely to be automated and will be essential for future job roles. Additionally, education systems must be flexible and adaptable, providing opportunities for lifelong learning and reskilling to keep pace with technological advancements.

The role of leadership and organizational culture is critical in navigating the transition to an automated and AI-driven workplace. Leaders must embrace a forward-thinking approach, recognizing the potential of these technologies while also addressing the challenges they pose. This involves fostering a culture of innovation, agility, and continuous improvement. Leaders must also prioritize the well-being and development of their workforce, ensuring that employees are supported through the transition and that their contributions are recognized and valued.

Chapter 37: Corporate Hierarchies

Corporate hierarchies have long been a defining feature of organizational structures, dictating the distribution of power, responsibilities, and rewards within companies. These hierarchies, while essential for maintaining order and efficiency in large organizations, often create a dynamic reminiscent of the historical relationships between masters and servants. As we delve into the intricacies of corporate hierarchies, it becomes clear how the power dynamics, social stratification, and sometimes exploitative practices mirror those seen in past systems of servitude. This examination reveals both the enduring nature of hierarchical power relations and the unique ways they manifest in the modern corporate world.

At the top of corporate hierarchies sit the executives, including CEOs, CFOs, and other C-suite leaders. These individuals wield significant power, making strategic decisions that shape the direction and success of the company. Their high status is often reflected in substantial salaries, bonuses, stock options, and other perks that vastly outstrip the compensation of lower-level employees. This concentration of wealth and power can create a stark divide between executives and the rest of the workforce, reinforcing a master-servant dynamic where those at the top enjoy privileges and influence far beyond the reach of their subordinates.

Beneath the executive level are middle managers, who serve as intermediaries between the upper echelons of leadership and the rank-and-file employees. Middle managers are tasked with implementing the strategic decisions made by executives and ensuring that day-to-day operations align with corporate goals. This layer of the hierarchy plays a crucial role in maintaining order and efficiency within the organization, but it can also be a source of tension and pressure. Middle managers often face the dual challenge of meeting the demands of their superiors while managing the expectations and performance of their teams. This intermediary position can create stress and a sense of servitude, as managers must navigate the demands from above and the needs from below.

At the base of the hierarchy are the rank-and-file employees, who perform the essential tasks that keep the company running. These workers, often seen as the "servants" in this dynamic, are typically subject to strict supervision, performance metrics, and limited autonomy. Their work is often characterized by repetitive tasks, rigid schedules, and a lack of decision-making power. The significant gap in compensation, job security, and influence between these employees and their higher-ups can lead to feelings of disenfranchisement and exploitation, mirroring the experiences of servants in historical contexts.

One of the most striking aspects of modern corporate hierarchies is the power dynamics that perpetuate inequality and control. Executives and top managers hold the authority to make decisions that affect the livelihoods of thousands of employees, from hiring and firing to determining wages and working conditions. This concentration of power can lead to abuses, such as unfair labor practices, discrimination, and exploitation. The fear of losing one's job can compel employees to endure poor working conditions, long hours, and inadequate pay, reinforcing their subordinate status within the hierarchy.

The psychological impact of corporate hierarchies is another important consideration. The clear delineation of roles and statuses can create a culture of deference and submission, where lower-level employees feel compelled to comply with the demands and expectations of their superiors. This dynamic can stifle creativity, innovation, and morale, as workers may feel that their contributions are undervalued or ignored. The constant pressure to meet performance targets and the lack of autonomy can lead to stress, burnout, and a sense of helplessness, further entrenching the master-servant relationship.

Corporate hierarchies also influence social interactions and relationships within the workplace. The division between higher and lower ranks can create social barriers that inhibit communication and collaboration. Executives and managers may be perceived as unapproachable or out of touch with the realities faced by frontline workers. This social stratification can lead to a lack of trust and mutual respect, undermining the sense of community and shared purpose that is essential for a healthy organizational culture. The social distance between different levels of the hierarchy can also perpetuate stereotypes and biases, further entrenching inequality and division.

The issue of pay disparity within corporate hierarchies is a significant factor in the master-servant dynamic. The enormous gap between executive compensation and the wages of rank-and-file employees is a source of ongoing controversy and criticism. While executives receive multi-million-dollar packages, stock options, and other benefits, many lower-level employees struggle with stagnant wages, limited benefits, and job insecurity. This stark contrast in compensation highlights the unequal distribution of wealth and power within corporations, reinforcing the hierarchical divide and perpetuating economic inequality.

Corporate hierarchies are also maintained and reinforced through systems of surveillance and control. Modern technology allows companies to monitor employee performance, productivity, and even behavior in unprecedented ways. From tracking software and performance metrics to video surveillance and biometric data, these tools can create a pervasive sense of being watched and evaluated. This constant surveillance can be dehumanizing, reducing employees to mere data points and reinforcing their subordinate status. The use of such technologies can also exacerbate power imbalances, as those at the top have access to detailed information about their subordinates while remaining largely unmonitored themselves.

Despite these challenges, corporate hierarchies are not inherently negative. They can provide structure, clarity, and efficiency, enabling large organizations to function effectively. The challenge lies in ensuring that these hierarchies do not become oppressive or exploitative. This requires a commitment to ethical leadership, equitable practices, and a focus on the well-being and development of all employees. Organizations that prioritize transparency, fairness, and employee engagement can mitigate the negative aspects of hierarchical structures and foster a more inclusive and supportive work environment.

One approach to addressing the negative impacts of corporate hierarchies is through the adoption of flatter organizational structures. Flatter hierarchies reduce the number of management levels, promoting greater autonomy, collaboration, and communication among employees. By empowering workers and involving them in decision-making processes, organizations can create a more inclusive and dynamic work environment. Flatter structures can also help to break down the social and psychological barriers that often accompany traditional hierarchies, fostering a sense of shared purpose and mutual respect.

Another important strategy is the promotion of ethical leadership. Leaders who prioritize the well-being of their employees, demonstrate integrity, and lead by example can create a positive organizational culture that mitigates the negative aspects of hierarchies. Ethical leaders are committed to fairness, transparency, and accountability, and they actively work to build trust and engagement within their teams. By fostering a culture of respect and inclusion, ethical leaders can help to balance the power dynamics inherent in corporate hierarchies and ensure that all employees are valued and supported.

The implementation of fair and equitable compensation practices is also crucial. Organizations must address the significant disparities in pay and benefits that contribute to the master-servant dynamic.

This includes not only providing fair wages but also ensuring that all employees have access to benefits such as healthcare, retirement plans, and professional development opportunities. Transparent and equitable compensation practices can help to reduce economic inequality and foster a more inclusive and supportive work environment.

Employee empowerment and engagement are key to mitigating the negative impacts of corporate hierarchies. Organizations that involve employees in decision-making processes, provide opportunities for professional growth, and recognize and reward contributions can create a more dynamic and motivated workforce. Empowered employees are more likely to feel valued and respected, reducing the sense of subordination and fostering a positive organizational culture. Engaging employees in meaningful work and providing opportunities for career advancement can also help to break down the hierarchical divide and promote a sense of shared purpose.

Chapter 38: The Cost of Success

The pursuit of success often demands a high price, and one of the most significant costs is the sacrifice of family and social life. This phenomenon, deeply embedded in modern society, is driven by a relentless ambition to achieve professional and financial milestones. The narrative of success, while alluring, conceals the profound personal and emotional toll it exacts on individuals and their relationships.

In the contemporary corporate world, the expectation to work extended hours has become the norm rather than the exception. The traditional 9-to-5 workday has stretched into the evening and often the weekend, encroaching on time that would otherwise be spent with family and friends. Employees find themselves tethered to their jobs, constantly accessible via smartphones and emails, which blurs the boundaries between work and personal life. This omnipresence of work commitments leaves little room for meaningful interactions with loved ones.

Micromanagement, a prevalent practice in many organizations, exacerbates this issue. Managers who closely monitor and control every aspect of their employees' work create an environment of constant pressure and scrutiny. This leads to heightened stress levels and the feeling of being perpetually on call. The need to meet stringent deadlines and exceed performance expectations often requires employees to sacrifice their evenings, weekends, and even vacations, leaving little time for rest and personal pursuits.

The psychological impact of this work culture is profound. Chronic stress and burnout are common among professionals who strive to balance demanding careers with personal lives. The relentless pursuit of success can lead to mental health issues such as anxiety and depression. The emotional exhaustion from constant work pressure often results in strained relationships with family and friends. Individuals may find themselves physically present but emotionally distant, unable to fully engage with their loved ones due to work-related stress and fatigue.

The sacrifice of family life in the name of success also has long-term implications. Children of parents who are perpetually preoccupied with their careers may experience feelings of neglect and abandonment. The lack of parental presence during crucial developmental stages can affect their emotional and psychological well-being. Spouses may feel isolated and undervalued, leading to marital discord and, in some cases, separation or divorce. The absence of a strong support system at home can leave individuals feeling lonely and disconnected, despite their professional achievements.

Social life, too, takes a significant hit. The demanding nature of modern work leaves little time for social engagements and leisure activities. Friendships often fall by the wayside as work commitments take precedence. Social isolation becomes a reality for many, as the time and energy required to maintain personal relationships are consumed by professional obligations. The loss of social connections can lead to a sense of loneliness and diminish overall life satisfaction.

Furthermore, the societal glorification of success and productivity perpetuates this cycle. There is a pervasive belief that success is measured by professional accomplishments and financial gains, often at the expense of personal well-being. This cultural narrative pressures individuals to prioritize their careers above all else, reinforcing the notion that sacrificing family and social life is a necessary trade-off for achieving success.

However, this relentless pursuit of success at the cost of personal life is not sustainable. The long-term consequences include deteriorating mental and physical health, weakened family bonds, and eroded social networks. Recognizing the need for a balanced approach to work and personal life is crucial. Organizations can play a pivotal role in this by fostering a culture that values work-life balance, providing flexible work arrangements, and promoting mental health and well-being.

Individuals, too, must take proactive steps to reclaim their personal lives. Setting clear boundaries between work and home, prioritizing self-care, and dedicating time to family and social activities are essential. Learning to say no to excessive work demands and seeking support from colleagues and loved ones can help mitigate the negative impacts of a demanding work environment.

Chapter 39: The Revolt of the Modern Worker

The modern worker's revolt, characterized by labor strikes and movements, is a powerful testament to the enduring struggle for fair treatment, better working conditions, and equitable compensation. Rooted in centuries of labor activism, these modern movements reflect the ongoing tensions between workers and employers in an increasingly complex and globalized economy. From the factory floors of the Industrial Revolution to the digital workspaces of the 21st century, the demands and tactics of labor movements have evolved, but their core purpose remains steadfast: to ensure that workers' rights and voices are respected and protected.

Labor strikes and movements have a long and storied history. During the Industrial Revolution, as workers faced grueling conditions, low wages, and long hours, they began organizing to demand better treatment. These early efforts were often met with fierce resistance from employers and sometimes even the state. Strikes were a common tactic, serving as a powerful means for workers to collectively assert their demands by halting production and disrupting business operations. Over time, these movements achieved significant victories, including the establishment of the eight-hour workday, safer working conditions, and the right to unionize.

In the modern era, labor strikes and movements have adapted to the changing landscape of work. The rise of technology, the gig economy, and globalization have introduced new challenges and opportunities for workers. Today, labor movements are as likely to be organized through social media and digital platforms as through traditional union halls. Workers in diverse sectors, from fast food and retail to technology and education, have mobilized to address issues such as wage theft, job insecurity, and inadequate benefits.

One of the most significant trends in recent labor movements is the resurgence of strikes and walkouts. For example, the Fight for $15 movement, which began in 2012, has been instrumental in advocating for higher wages for fast food and low-wage workers. This movement has utilized strikes and protests to draw attention to the plight of workers earning below a livable wage. Their efforts have resulted in tangible successes, including wage increases in several states and municipalities, and have inspired similar campaigns globally.

Teachers have also been at the forefront of modern labor movements. In recent years, educators across the United States have organized large-scale strikes to demand better pay, improved classroom conditions, and increased funding for public schools. These strikes, often supported by parents and communities, highlight the critical role of teachers and the importance of investing in education. The success of these movements has brought national attention to the challenges faced by educators and has led to significant policy changes in several states.

The tech industry, once seen as a bastion of progressive workplace culture, has also witnessed a wave of labor activism. Workers at major tech companies like Google, Amazon, and Microsoft have organized protests and walkouts to address issues ranging from sexual harassment and discrimination to unethical business practices and poor working conditions. These actions have not only challenged the internal policies of these companies but have also sparked broader discussions about the power dynamics in the tech industry and the need for greater corporate accountability.

Gig economy workers, such as those driving for ride-sharing companies or delivering food, have also begun to organize. These workers often face precarious employment conditions, lacking benefits, job security, and fair wages. Through strikes, protests, and legal challenges, gig workers are fighting for recognition as employees rather than independent contractors, which would grant them greater protections and benefits. Their struggle is emblematic of the broader challenges faced by workers in an economy that increasingly favors flexibility and short-term contracts over stable, long-term employment.

The COVID-19 pandemic has further intensified labor activism. As essential workers faced heightened risks without adequate protection or compensation, many organized strikes and protests to demand safer working conditions, hazard pay, and better health benefits. The pandemic underscored the essential nature of many low-wage jobs and the need for systemic changes to ensure that all workers are treated with dignity and respect.

Internationally, labor movements have taken on diverse forms to address local and global issues. In countries with emerging economies, workers often contend with exploitative conditions reminiscent of the early Industrial Revolution. Strikes and labor protests in places like Bangladesh's garment factories or China's manufacturing hubs highlight the global struggle for workers' rights. These movements are crucial in advocating for fair wages, safe working conditions, and the right to organize.

Labor movements also intersect with broader social justice issues. For instance, the intersection of labor rights with racial and gender equality has gained prominence, as movements recognize that marginalized groups often face compounded challenges in the workplace. The push for inclusive and equitable labor practices is an integral part of modern labor activism, reflecting a more holistic approach to worker rights.

Despite significant progress, modern labor movements face numerous challenges. Anti-union sentiments, legal obstacles, and the changing nature of work pose significant hurdles. Many employers resist unionization efforts, and labor laws in various regions may not fully protect the rights of workers to organize and strike. Additionally, the rise of automation and artificial intelligence presents new uncertainties for the future of work, potentially displacing millions of jobs and altering the landscape of labor activism.

Nevertheless, the resilience and adaptability of labor movements offer hope for the future. As workers continue to organize and advocate for their rights, they build on a legacy of solidarity and struggle. The power of collective action remains a potent force for change, capable of challenging injustices and securing a more equitable and humane workplace.

Chapter 40: Breaking the Chains

Creating a fair and equitable workplace is a complex and multifaceted challenge, requiring concerted efforts from individuals, organizations, and policymakers. It involves dismantling systemic inequalities, promoting diversity and inclusion, ensuring fair wages, and fostering a culture of respect and dignity for all workers. This journey towards equity in the workplace is not only a moral imperative but also a strategic necessity for the sustainability and success of businesses and economies in the modern world.

One of the foundational aspects of a fair and equitable workplace is the establishment of fair wages. Wage disparities have long been a source of inequality, with significant gaps often existing between different genders, races, and job categories. Addressing this issue requires transparent pay structures and regular audits to ensure that compensation is based on merit and performance rather than discriminatory practices. The implementation of living wages, which reflect the actual cost of living, is crucial in ensuring that all workers can afford basic necessities and live with dignity.

Moreover, wage transparency is a powerful tool in combating pay inequality. By openly sharing salary ranges and criteria for pay increases, organizations can reduce the opportunity for bias and discrimination. This transparency not only builds trust among employees but also holds organizations accountable for maintaining fair pay practices. Legislation mandating pay transparency, coupled with robust enforcement mechanisms, can further drive progress in this area.

Diversity and inclusion are also essential components of a fair and equitable workplace. A diverse workforce brings a wealth of perspectives and experiences, fostering innovation and creativity. However, diversity alone is not enough; inclusion ensures that all employees feel valued and empowered to contribute fully. This requires a proactive approach to dismantling barriers that prevent marginalized groups from advancing in their careers.

To promote diversity and inclusion, organizations must implement comprehensive policies and programs. This includes targeted recruitment efforts to attract a diverse pool of candidates, as well as ongoing training and development opportunities to support the career growth of underrepresented groups. Mentorship and sponsorship programs can be particularly effective in providing guidance and support to employees from diverse backgrounds, helping them navigate their career paths and overcome obstacles.

Inclusive leadership is another critical factor. Leaders who actively champion diversity and inclusion set the tone for the entire organization. They must be willing to challenge the status quo, address biases, and create an environment where all employees feel safe and respected. This involves not only verbal commitment but also concrete actions, such as setting diversity goals, measuring progress, and holding themselves and their teams accountable for achieving these goals.

Creating a fair and equitable workplace also necessitates addressing the systemic inequalities that exist within organizational structures and processes. This includes revising recruitment, promotion, and performance evaluation practices to ensure they are free from bias. Blind recruitment processes, for instance, can help eliminate unconscious bias by removing identifying information from applications. Similarly, standardized evaluation criteria can ensure that performance assessments are based on objective measures rather than subjective opinions.

Work-life balance is another critical aspect of an equitable workplace. Employees should have the flexibility to balance their professional responsibilities with personal commitments. This involves offering flexible work arrangements, such as remote work options, flexible hours, and parental leave policies that support both mothers and fathers. By recognizing the diverse needs of employees and accommodating them, organizations can create a more inclusive and supportive work environment.

Health and well-being are also integral to a fair and equitable workplace. Employers must prioritize the physical and mental health of their employees by providing comprehensive health benefits, access to wellness programs, and a supportive environment that encourages work-life balance. Addressing issues such as workplace stress, burnout, and harassment is essential in fostering a healthy and productive workforce. Mental health support, including access to counseling and mental health days, should be a standard part of employee benefits.

Furthermore, fostering a culture of respect and dignity is crucial in creating an equitable workplace. This involves zero tolerance for any form of discrimination, harassment, or bullying. Organizations must establish clear policies and procedures for reporting and addressing such issues, ensuring that employees feel safe and supported in speaking out. Regular training on topics such as unconscious bias, cultural competence, and respectful communication can help create a more inclusive and respectful work environment.

Employee participation and voice are also key elements of an equitable workplace. Workers should have the opportunity to participate in decision-making processes that affect their work and working conditions. This can be achieved through various mechanisms, such as employee representation on boards, regular feedback surveys, and open forums for discussion. By involving employees in these processes, organizations can foster a sense of ownership and empowerment, leading to greater job satisfaction and productivity.

In addition to internal efforts, collaboration with external stakeholders is essential in promoting workplace equity. This includes partnering with community organizations, advocacy groups, and other businesses to share best practices and drive broader societal change. Industry-wide initiatives and standards can help set benchmarks for fair and equitable practices, encouraging organizations to strive for continuous improvement.

Policy advocacy is another critical aspect of this journey. Governments play a crucial role in setting and enforcing labor standards that promote fairness and equity. This includes implementing and upholding anti-discrimination laws, mandating equal pay for equal work, and ensuring safe and healthy working conditions. Advocacy efforts aimed at influencing public policy can help create a more equitable labor market and level the playing field for all workers.

Finally, measuring and reporting progress is essential in the pursuit of workplace equity. Organizations should regularly assess their diversity, inclusion, and equity efforts, using metrics and benchmarks to track progress and identify areas for improvement. Transparent reporting on these efforts not only demonstrates a commitment to equity but also holds organizations accountable to their employees, stakeholders, and the broader community.

Epilogue

As we turn the final page of "Chains Through Centuries: From Ancient Slavery to Modern Workplaces," we stand at a critical juncture, reflecting on the long and winding path humanity has traversed. Our journey through the epochs of history reveals a persistent thread of subjugation and struggle, but also of resilience and the relentless pursuit of freedom.

The story of slavery and control is not merely a historical account; it is a mirror reflecting the ongoing challenges we face in contemporary society. While the overt brutality of ancient slavery has largely receded, modern forms of bondage persist, subtly entwining themselves into the fabric of our daily lives. The corporate world, with its demands and pressures, often replicates the dynamics of old, reminding us that the chains of control have not been entirely broken but merely transformed.

Yet, there is hope. History has shown us that human dignity and the quest for liberation are powerful forces capable of transcending even the most entrenched systems of oppression. The abolition movements, labor unions, and modern advocates for workers' rights exemplify the enduring spirit of resistance and the drive for a more equitable world.

As we contemplate the lessons from the past, it becomes evident that progress is neither linear nor guaranteed. It requires constant vigilance, awareness, and action. The fight against modern forms of exploitation—whether in sweatshops, through human trafficking, or within the confines of a toxic workplace—demands our attention and our commitment.

The digital age presents new challenges and opportunities. Automation and artificial intelligence threaten to reshape the landscape of work once again, potentially leading to unprecedented levels of unemployment and inequality. However, these technological advancements also offer the potential to liberate us from the drudgery of repetitive tasks, allowing for a reimagining of what meaningful work can be.

In envisioning a future free from the chains of the past, we must prioritize human well-being over profit, advocate for policies that ensure fair treatment and opportunities for all, and cultivate workplaces that respect and nurture the individual. This future hinges on our collective ability to learn from history, to recognize the enduring patterns of power and control, and to break the cycles of exploitation that persist.

"Chains Through Centuries" is a call to action. It urges us to acknowledge the resilience of those who came before us, to honor their struggles, and to continue their fight for justice. It is an invitation to engage with the present critically and to shape a future where freedom, dignity, and equity are the hallmarks of our shared human experience.

As we close this book, let us carry forward its lessons. Let us be vigilant against the subtle forms of bondage that pervade our modern world and strive tirelessly for a society where the chains of oppression are finally and irrevocably broken. Our journey is far from over, but with awareness and action, we can move towards a world where every individual is truly free.

The End.